AN INVITATION TO QUALITATIVE FIELDWORK

An Invitation to Qualitative Fieldwork uniquely provides a complete picture of qualitative methods by explaining both the "why to" and the "how to," offering both the theory and practical "recipes" for how to do qualitative research. Qualitative methods have become so diverse that it is easy to feel bewildered by their variety and overwhelmed by the increasingly detailed body of knowledge. In response, this book invites students to try their hand at qualitative fieldwork, using straightforward language and examples that prove anyone can succeed in collecting valuable qualitative data. This is an ideal text for any course on qualitative research.

Jason Orne has a PhD in Sociology from the University of Wisconsin-Madison. His ethnography, *Boystown,* is under contract with the University of Chicago Press. It traces the racial and sexual consequences of late-stage gentrification in a gay neighborhood. His academic work has been featured in the journals *Sexualities* and *The Sociological Quarterly*. His creative nonfiction work is in a variety of venues, from the magazine *The Morning News* to the anthology *Off the Rocks*.

Michael M. Bell is Vilas Distinguished Achievement Professor of Community and Environmental Sociology and Director of the Center for Integrated Agricultural Systems at the University of Wisconsin-Madison. Mike is also an ethnographer, agroecologist, and social theorist. He is an author or editor of eight other books, including two award-winning ethnographies. In 1994 he published *Childerley: Nature and Morality in a Country Village* (University of Chicago Press, 1994), which was co-winner of the 1995 Best Book Award of the Sociology of Culture Section of the American Sociological Association. Ten years later he finished his second ethnography, *Farming for Us All: Practical Agriculture and the Cultivation of Sustainability* (Penn State University Press, 2004), which won an Outstanding Academic Title Award from the American Library Association. He is currently conducting participatory fieldwork among the amaQwathi people of the Eastern Cape Province of South Africa.

Mike has a musical second life as a composer and performer. His compositions include pieces for solo piano, symphony orchestra, and various chamber ensembles, as well as numerous "class-grass" works—a hybrid of bluegrass and classical traditions. He frequently performs on mandolin and banjo with the Madison-based class-grass ensemble *Graminy* (www.graminy.net).

Titles of Related Interest

Ethnography and the City: Readings on Doing Urban Fieldwork
Edited by Richard E. Ocejo

Re-Imagining Milk: Culture and Biological Perspectives
Andrea Wiley

Coffee Culture: Local Experiences, Global Connections
Catherine M. Tucker

Lycra: How a Fiber Shaped America
Kaori O'Connor

Fake Stuff: China and the Rise of Counterfeit Goods
Yi-Chieh Jessica Lin

The World of Wal-Mart: Discounting the American Dream
Nick Copeland & Christine Labuski

Alcohol: Social Drinking in Cultural Context
Janet Chrzan

Reconsidering the Bicycle: An Anthropological Perspective on a New (Old) Thing
Luis A. Vivanco

Ferry Tales: Mobility, Place, and Time on Canada's West Coast
Phillip Vannini

Digital Drama: Teaching and Learning Art and Media in Tanzania
Paula Uimonen

Concrete and Dust: Mapping the Sexual Terrains of Los Angeles
Jeanine Marie Minge & Amber Lynn Zimmerman

Water in a Dry Land: Place-Learning through Art and Story
Margaret Somerville

My Father's Wars: Migration, Memory, and the Violence of Century
Alisse Waterston

Beads, Bodies, and Trash: Public Sex, Global Labor, and the Disposability of Mardi Gras
David Redmon

Off the Grid: Re-Assembling Domestic Life
Phillip Vannini & Jonathan Taggart

In Solidarity: Friendship, Family, and Activist Beyond Gay and Straight
Lisa Tillmann

Forthcoming:

Global Cities, Local Streets: Social Spaces of Everyday Diversity
Edited by Sharon Zukin, Philip Kasinitz, & Xiangming Chen

AN INVITATION TO QUALITATIVE FIELDWORK

A Multilogical Approach

Jason Orne
Michael M. Bell

All images by Matthew Raboin

NEW YORK AND LONDON

First published 2015
by Routledge
711 Third Avenue, New York, NY 10017

and by Routledge
2 Park Square, Milton Park, Abingdon, Oxon, OX14 4RN

Routledge is an imprint of the Taylor & Francis Group, an informa business

Library of Congress Cataloging-in-Publication Data
Orne, Jason.
An invitation to qualitative fieldwork : a multilogical approach / by Jason Orne & Michael M. Bell.
pages cm
Includes bibliographical references and index.
1. Social sciences—Fieldwork. 2. Social sciences—Research—Methodology.
I. Bell, Michael M. II. Title.
H62.O745 2015
001.4'33—dc23
2014032657

ISBN: 978-0-415-53661-5 (hbk)
ISBN: 978-0-415-53662-2 (pbk)
ISBN: 978-1-315-79416-7 (ebk)

Typeset in Caslon Pro
by ApexCovantage, LLC

Printed and bound in the United States of America
by Edwards Brothers Malloy

Contents in Brief

Contents in Detail

PREFACE

What is there left to say about qualitative methods? Once seen as the realm of outlaws and bohemians, qualitative research is now an accepted and prominent feature of the academic landscape. Indeed, our own academic library lists hundreds of books about qualitative methodology. Do we really need another one?

We believe, yes, we really do. There is more to say, much more, precisely because so many scholars are now talking about qualitative research. The endeavor is growing rapidly and lushly, with a wide range of new cultivars, polymorphs, and offshoots. Indeed, qualitative methods have become so diverse that it is easy to feel bewildered by its variety and overwhelmed by its increasingly detailed body of knowledge. Even experienced qualitative fieldworkers sometimes feel left behind and confused, kind of like a parent of a teenager, befuddled and maybe even alarmed by the latest cultural trends.

That's why we titled this book *An Invitation to Qualitative Fieldwork*. We mean it to be a welcome to students, novices, and rookies to try their hand at qualitative fieldwork. And we mean it to be a re-invitation for those looking for a refresher. We seek to provide a clear language for thinking about fieldwork, along with practical tips for making it happen. As we describe in chapter 1, we think of this invitation as a kind of cooking book—a work that explains both the "why to" and "how to" of qualitative cooking, both the theory of qualitative research and practical "recipes" for how to do it. Such an approach we hope will be inviting to those feeling a bit scared by all the stuff that we have now in the cabinets and drawers of the qualitative kitchen.

Fieldwork sometimes has a mystique, as though it takes a special kind of person, someone more adventurous or outgoing than many of us. It really only takes a special set of skills and enough knowledge of the logics those skills embody to be able to adapt them to the unique circumstances of every fieldwork project. By blending practical advice and exercises with more philosophical considerations, our book aims to teach the skills and knowledge needed to cook up a fieldwork project from inception to fruition.

As such, this book can be used in two ways. Read it in order, learning about the different methods and perspectives of qualitative fieldwork from conception to dissemination. Alternatively, if you have a question on a particular topic—consent forms?—or want to practice a skill—ethnographic observation?—skip around. The index is thorough and complete, filled with references to where you can find skills, topics, and other practical matters that the book covers.

The kitchen of social context is infinitely complex. But there is no need to make what comes out of it bland and dull, because of some sense that we need to simplify its possibilities. Through fieldwork, we can embrace that complexity and the multiple logics it manifests. We can make a social science cuisine that is tasty, nutritious, fulfilling, and diverse. And it doesn't have to be difficult. We hope in this book to show how, using multilogical methods for a multilogical world.

* * *

Like the multilogical methods that we use, this book also has multiple voices, from which we have joint and individual thanks to give. As authors, Jason and Mike developed this book and the multilogical frame, first through their work together as mentee and mentor, student and teacher, like perhaps many of the readers of this book. But eventually as colleagues and friends, as we hope many of our readers will soon be.

In this way, the book's antecedents are our shared methodological history, but also those who taught each of us methods. Jason thanks Gloria Gonzalez-Lopez, Cameron Macdonald, Richard and Mary-Anne Casey, and Mike. Mike thanks Kai Erikson, James Scott, Sandra Wallman, Mitch Duneier, and Jason. We also couldn't have written this book without the students at University of Wisconsin-Madison, who were often the first to sample our recipes. The multilogical perspective also grew out of a book by Mike, his 2011 Temple University Press volume *The Strange Music of Social Life*, which came out of a conversation with ten other scholars, whom he thanks for their insightful contributions.

Neither of us would have had insights into method without the fieldwork that we conducted previously and the strange lessons that participants teach us. Mike's work in the pseudonymous English village Childerley, the literal fields of Iowa, and off the beaten path in South Africa provided field-tested methods of producing scholarly work, often with real impact on the lives of those communities participating. Jason's lessons, in the essays and interviews with young gay men and women and in the nightclubs of Boystown, a Chicago neighborhood, were a jolt and sometimes a break from the past. Today's qualitative fieldwork incorporates every voice, way of gathering, and method of communication.

This book would not be in your hands without the steady encouragement—and pokes and prods—from our editor at Routledge, Stephen Rutter. Thank you for your faith in the project over its years of inception. We're especially grateful for the comments made on earlier drafts by colleagues, who include:

Heather Jacobson	University of Texas at Arlington
Patricia Maloney	Texas Tech University
Bryan Sykes	University of California, Irvine
Anastasia Vogt-Yuan	Virginia Tech
Carol Bailey	Virginia Tech
Corey Colyer	West Virginia University
Simon Gottschalk	University of Nevada, Las Vegas
Christian Churchill	St. Thomas Aquinas College
Jane Hood	University of New Mexico
Donna Bird	University of Southern Maine
Debra Branch	Southern Methodist University
Ronald Mize	Oregon State University
Kenneth Kolb	Furman University
Beth Duckles	Bucknell University

Neither of us could have written this volume without the support of family. Jason's husband, Austin Duus, and Mike's wife, Diane Mayerfeld, are stalwart partners in the kitchens of our own home lives.

And lastly, we thank you, the reader, for picking up this book, accepting our invitation to have a go at cooking up the complex and flavorful dishes of qualitative field work.

bama himself as an
ample, and the victory speech he gav
at evening in Chicago's Grant Park to a crow
f over 200,000, plus millions more on television.
n the context of this election, we can justly imagine th
he saw himself in many ways at once: as a Democrat; as
a middle-aged man; as the first African-American to be elec
president; as a grandson whose grandmother had passed awa
only two days prior to the election; as a father and husband wh
ould have to navigate family life amid the constraints of living
n the White House; as th
trigues and schemes.
the hopes and dreams, and t
ome of which he no do
ple and their varied intere
Obama himself could te
re obligatory than just.
oment for him, if he wo
ut the contextuality of t
nd there was much mo
terview on the subject.
e probably could not s
tuality of that moment
ave had, complete access
not have, nor could h
nd millions.
same w
lity for those million
here is alwa
social situation
n it, inc
involve
bout.

1
THE MULTILOGICAL APPROACH

The "job talk" is one of the great rites of academic passage. Candidates spend hours honing what usually represents years of work into a 45 or 50-minute presentation. They worry about what to include. They fuss with the layout of the slides. They stand in front of the mirror trying out different outfits. They practice in front of friends and mentors. They struggle to sleep well the night beforehand.

Mike had endured all that (including the struggle to sleep well). And he had just finished giving the real thing, the actual job talk, at a prestigious East Coast university. He thought the presentation went great. The talk clocked in right on the money at 45 minutes, and Mike made hardly a verbal stumble. So he was feeling good. But nevertheless a little anxious too: The talk was for a position he desperately wanted.

Mike was confident about his argument, drawn from a chapter of his dissertation, an ethnography of the meaning of nature among the residents of an exurban village in England. He thought he had a tight academic case about the relationship between social class and whether villagers thought fox-hunting—a controversial blood sport which the British parliament later banned—was cruel. Middle-class villagers thought fox-hunting was cruel if they were politically left, and thought it wasn't if they were politically right. Regardless of their party and politics, working-class villagers also thought it was cruel, unless they were (or a close relative was) employed by the fox-hunt. Mike hadn't found a single exception to these patterns in his fieldwork, which supported the larger theoretical point he was trying to establish about how ideas of nature reflected social ideas.

Mike put down his notes, flashed a smile at the classroom of professors and students, and asked, "Are there any questions?"

Immediately, a hand went up in the back corner of the room.

"Yes?" Mike invited.

A grey-haired man wearing a tweed blazer lumbered to his feet.

("Uh-oh," thought Mike.)

"Mister Bell," began the grey-haired man.

("'Mister Bell'? Uh-oh for sure . . . .")

"I have only one question for you. In what way would you distinguish your work from fiction?"

Needless to say, Mike didn't get that job. He did get an academic job eventually (and even published his dissertation at an academic press).[1] Otherwise we probably would not have been given the chance to write this book. We also would not have written it if stories like this—stories that show a continuing doubt in some quarters about qualitative fieldwork methods and a corresponding defensiveness among its practitioners—weren't still so common.[2] The situation has much improved in our own field, sociology, since Mike gave that ill-fated talk in 1992. Qualitative fieldwork is now regularly accepted in most of the leading sociology journals and a sociology department with no qualitative methodologists would be considered odd. Geography and education departments are also now generally welcoming of qualitative fieldwork and anthropology always has been. The situation remains more mixed, however, in political science, economics, business, psychology, and the health sciences.

We offer this book to aspiring qualitative fieldworkers in all fields. We offer it both to those seeking to improve their understanding and practice of qualitative fieldwork and to those seeking to persuade others of its value. We offer it, too, as a new synthesis of qualitative fieldwork as a ***contextual science**** attuned to the *multiple logics* of any instance of social life—and the relations, interactions, constraints, histories, regularities, and creative surprises that shape these logics and that these logics afford.

---

* Find the definitions of all bolded terms in the Glossary Index.

Contextuality and Intercontextuality

Consider the context of Mike's ill-fated job talk. The meanings and consequences of Mike's talk were highly contingent on how those in the room understood it—on the logic (really, the logics) they brought to bear on the talk and how the context of the talk encouraged or discouraged various logics for evaluating it. Most obviously, the talk's success depended in part on how well Mike met the standards of academic performance. Did he speak well? Did he dress well? Were the slides nicely done? Was there an appropriate mix of theory and evidence? Did he clearly connect the work to important academic questions and literatures? Did it seem to offer something new?

But given that Mike did eventually get a job using this same talk (albeit with a few modifications), we can assume the relative success of the talk was not contingent on Mike's performance alone. Other logics also danced around in the context. Not necessarily logical logics, however—at least from Mike's point of view! The logicalness of any particular logic in our multi-logical world is something we may all have different opinions about. At the very least, the grey-haired man understood the talk quite differently from how Mike did.

Fortunately, although that questioner did not trust Mike's ethnography, many others did. No one else asked him a direct question like that (thankfully, says Mike). He did get many other questions, of course, each one a consequence of how someone understood what Mike had presented and why they were attending his talk. Graduate students who were pondering their own future job talks responded differently than faculty members with votes in the selection process. Undergraduates attending for extra credit points in a course took it differently again. Everyone brings at least a different logic to a situation. There were as well differences of subdisciplinary interest, theoretical predilection, and personal political views. Given our usual social concern for matters of gender, sexuality, class, race, age, looks, and so much more, audience members probably also considered Mike's presentation in light of how they identified themselves and how they identified Mike with regard to these characteristics, even if subconsciously. More logics yet.

But these varying reactions did also depend upon Mike. People from different universities were responding to what he—a wavy-haired white male then in his early thirties, exhibiting the class competencies of many years of university training—said about a topic not commonly dissected by American academics: British fox-hunting. Likely, most people in those lecture rooms had never heard a talk on British fox-hunting—and assuredly not one delivered by Mike. These talks were situations that the people in them had never exactly encountered before, as familiar as most features of these situations no doubt were to them. And they responded to them in ways that differed at least a little bit from how they had responded to other talks they had experienced.

What everyday evidence like these varying reactions suggest to the qualitative fieldworker is that different people in different situations will understand differently and accordingly act differently. It also suggests that different people in the *same* situation will understand and act differently. We should put the matter more strongly: No one situation is ever the same for everyone in it, because of our differences.

Let's get this down as tightly as we can. One situation, many logics. Many situations, many, many logics.

In short, when we speak of context in this book, we don't mean uniformity of experience for all concerned. Nor do we mean that those in a context are leaves passively floating along a stream of social life. (Mike's questioner definitely diverted the flow of events.) People shape context and are shaped by it—a two-way effect we call the *contextuality* of a social situation.

Contextuality is infinitely complex—and we do mean "infinitely." We have only been scratching at the surface of understandings and actions elicited by, and involved in, Mike's job talks that year. Yes, it was all university people in university settings engaged in a familiar kind of university event. But the people involved had different histories, different concerns, different positions within the event. And while his particular job talk was much the same as any other (or people would not have recognized it as a job talk), it was also unlike any other. Indeed, if it had been exactly the same, and if everyone in it had responded in exactly the same way, those involved would probably have been deeply disturbed and questioned their own sanity. Life isn't like that.

So contextuality is not constancy. Not only does any one context contain potentially huge diversity within it, no one context is ever completely the same as another. Thus, given the variation and complexity of real life, a complete rendering of contexuality is beyond what science can achieve.

Perhaps it would be theoretically possible to render it completely, but practically speaking it could not be done.

Indeed, a strong case could be made that a complete rendering of contextuality is actually theoretically impossible—especially when we consider an event of far more consequence to far more people than Mike's talk so many years ago.

Consider the many meanings involved in the election of Barack Hussein Obama on November 4, 2008 to the office of President of the United States. Nearly 130 million people voted in that election. Many were overjoyed with the result. And many were not. Their reasons for approval or disapproval varied widely. Moreover, Obama's election had many meanings for most people involved in its context—not just one meaning per person, as our surface scratching up above perhaps implied. No doubt some meanings were more consequential than others for each person, but each still experienced a multitude.

Take Obama himself and the victory speech he gave that evening in Chicago's Grant Park to a crowd of over 200,000, plus millions more on television. Obama likely saw himself in many ways at once. As a Democrat. As a former US senator. As a middle-aged man. As the first African-American to be elected president. As a grandson whose grandmother had passed only two days prior to the election. As a father and husband who would have to navigate family life amid the constraints of the White House. As the bearer of the hopes and dreams—and the intrigues and schemes—of millions and millions of people, many of which he did not personally support, given the inevitable compromises of building a political coalition.

Obama himself could tell us much more about the contextuality of that moment for him if he would consent to an interview on the subject. And there was much about the contextuality of that moment he probably could not speak to, for he did not have, nor could not have had, complete access to its contextuality for those millions and millions. The same would be true of any social situation: There is always so much going on for every person involved in it, including much that they do not understand or know about.

One person, one situation, many logics.

Moreover, a person's involvements actually extend beyond any one situation, making a complete rendering of contextuality even more difficult. For we bring our lives with us wherever we go. What we do in any one place and moment has implications that stretch elsewhere and else when. The significance of a context lies in how it matters for more than that one spot in the continuum of space and time. Otherwise, why be bothered about what goes on in it?

Just as importantly, what happens in other situations far away in space and time shapes what happens in the situations of our own little struggles and enjoyments. Any one context almost always—and maybe really and truly always—has consequence for another.

In this book we refer to this interdependent consequence of context as ***intercontextuality***, the connection any one context has to many others. A contextual science must also be an intercontextual science, looking at the bigger in the smaller and the smaller in the bigger—or, to use terms often favored by social theorists, looking at the macro in the micro and the micro in the macro.

Take Obama's gender. As historic as his victory was from the perspective of race relations in the US, there was nothing novel in him becoming the 44th man in a row to be elected president. One would not have to be a deep student of social life to recognize that there is a long social history of assumptions and privileges associated with the distinctions we make between men and women, not least with regard to politics and power. The context of masculinity and patriarchy came into that speech at Grant Park and went on beyond it, reinforcing some presumptions about gender but also opening up others, given that Obama's main primary challenger had been a woman, Hilary Rodham Clinton—but a woman who had gained prominence to a significant degree because of her husband, President Bill Clinton.

Which is all a long way round to say that a social situation has a lot more going on than immediately meets the eye, and its implications extend from one situation to the next, ever varying and ever connecting.

A Multilogical Method for a Multilogical World

Researchers often seek a more unified and stable image of the empirical world than we have been describing here. But qualitative fieldwork typically does not yield such confidence—although not because of any necessary lack of accuracy. Rather, the closeness and detail of qualitative fieldwork give researchers a deep appreciation of the complications and contradictions of real social life. Thus, while the qualitative fieldworker seeks to understand the interdependent consequences of context, she or he does not imagine a seamless world that is all one vast weave of threads, webs, or wires. Social life is not *The Matrix*. There is no single Architect or Source, no unified master logic to which all must comply, aside from the occasional Anomaly. There are indeed important connections across space and time, as one context intercontextually reaches into others. We very much need to understand these connections, which we often have trouble seeing from the perspective of an individual life or locality. But the social is also replete with differences, conflicts, disconnections, and resistances. We need to pay equal attention to these disjunctures, and not necessarily with an eye to eliminating them or folding them into an ever-grander theory of everything. Very often it is the disjunctures which give us hope and opportunity, not merely dismay and confusion.[3]

Let's take another look at Obama's 2008 victory speech. His election was, of course, vigorously contested by his challenger, Senator John McCain. Although Obama won 68 percent of the Electoral College, the US's singular means of tabulating votes state by state, he received less than 53 percent of the popular vote. This outcome was far from clear over the course of the campaign. Only three months before the election, national polls had shown McCain with a ten-point lead. Both sides had reason to hope and both sides saw opportunity. Each side tried tactics that had not been used before. The Obama campaign used social media such as MySpace and Facebook that had barely even existed in the previous presidential election, raising an unprecedented level of contributions from small donors. John McCain chose as his running mate the first woman Republican vice presidential candidate, Governor Sarah Palin. Despite the increasing precision and frequency of polls, no one really knew how it would turn out until close to the end. There were simply too many logics of social life in play—too many intercontextually connected contexts, shaping and reshaping each other—for anyone to be sure.

Indeed, if everyone had known how the election would turn out, then it quite possibly would have turned out differently. Many citizens might have decided not to bother to vote—and most probably the non-voters would have been those for whom voting is the most difficult: students living away from home, people with limited transportation options, low-paid workers with second jobs, single parents with uncertain child-care support, and other likely Obama voters. Knowledge of what seems likely to happen leads people to adjust what they do, an outcome that political campaigners often struggle with. The predictableness of the world is often exactly what undermines the expected—and what can even enable us to subvert it.

Rather than imagining or seeking a single logic of social life, it seems more accurate, and thus ultimately more useful, to recognize that ours is a *multilogical world*.[4] To be sure, the social world has its zones of at least relatively well-unified logics that extend from person to person, space to space, and time to time. But there is not only one such relatively unified logic for any person, space, or time—or for all persons, spaces, and times. This multipleness is highly consequential. The differences in situation they stem from, and that they create, matter a lot for how we live.

If the world is multilogical, then we need modes of discovery that alert us and inform us about these differences. We offer this book's contextual (and intercontextual) method for the social sciences as one such mode.

Weber's Scar

One of the challenges of a multilogical world, and for any science that grapples with it, is that other people so commonly do things that seem stupid, odd, irrational, or even immoral to us. How do we understand another's various logics when they are so different from our own?

Consider the three-inch-long scar that the great sociologist Max Weber, one of the founding figures of the field, proudly sported on his left cheek. As a student at the University of Heidelberg in the early 1880s, Weber took up *akademisches Fechten*, or "academic fencing." For the German university students of the day, who were almost all male, academic fencing wasn't merely academic. Students fenced with real swords and wore no masks. Sometimes they fenced with no protection at all. The point was not to win, however. If anything, it was just the reverse: to show your courage by unflinchingly taking a *schmiss* (a smite) to the face so that you might gain a permanent scar that displayed your masculine prowess to all.

To most people today, fencing to get scars seems a bizarre practice. Yet it still goes on, albeit uncommonly, carried into the present by a few German university fraternities or *Studentenverbindung*. How can we understand it?

In his great work *Economy and Society*, Weber argued that "Sociology ... is a science which attempts the **interpretive understanding** of social action in order thereby to arrive at a causal explanation of its course and effects."[5] He distinguished between two forms of interpretive understanding, what he termed ***subjective understanding*** and ***explanatory understanding***. By subjective understanding, Weber meant understanding what someone does from that person's own perspective—understanding it as she or he understands it. We can gain subjective understanding either by observing the person's reactions, such as "an outbreak of anger as manifested by facial expression, exclamations or irrational movements," as Weber put it, or through hearing her or his own account of the action.[6] For example, here is Weber himself on what he got out of participating in *akademisches Fechten*:

> The usual training for haughty aggression in the dueling fraternity and as an officer has undoubtedly had a strong influence on me. It removed the shyness and insecurity of my adolescence.[7]

Explanatory understanding, though, requires something more. As Weber wrote, it requires the social scientist to "plac[e] the act in an intelligible and more inclusive context of meaning," and thereby to grasp it as "an understandable sequence of motivation."[8] Subjective understanding is about who and what; explanatory understanding is about why and where. Explanatory understanding, then, is contextual understanding—and therefore also intercontextual understanding. The social scientist's work is not complete until he or she gains both subjective and explanatory understanding. The social actor will likely be less inclined, and perhaps less able, to pursue explanatory understanding with as much care.

But the social actor is certainly able to engage in both subjective understanding and explanatory understanding as he or she seeks to interpret experiences. It would be inaccurate to neatly divide accounts of the social world into subjective understanding that the social actor possesses versus explanatory understanding that the social scientist possesses, or at least tries hard to attain. For example, Weber's account of his dueling (and military service) plainly contains not only subjective understanding but also an explanation: how the aggressiveness he learned helped him mature from a shy and insecure adolescent. A case could probably be made that there is at least some validity to Weber's explanation of his own dueling.[9]

But the social scientist looking at Weber's explanation might observe that there were more factors intercontextually at work in the context of *akademisches Fechten*. To name one, academic fencing is highly gendered. It is about men dueling men and men standing unflinching as they slice each other's foreheads and cheeks with the tips of their *Schlägers*, the special swords used in these duels. The "haughty aggression" that Weber praised was a characteristic that men were rewarded for having and socially punished for not having—and conversely for women. Much social scientific work shows that these same dynamics continue today in Germany and in Western culture more generally, although usually in more muted forms. But Weber as a social actor did not observe the gendered valuing of haughty aggression and how it supported patriarchal power.

Weber as a social scientist, however, recognized the possibility that the social actor may not completely "get it," even about his or her own context. Let's hear from Weber at length on this point:

> In the first place the "conscious motives" may well, even to the actor himself, conceal the various "motives" and "repressions" which constitute the real driving force of his action. Thus in such cases even subjectively honest self-analysis has only a relative value. Then it is the task of the sociologist to be aware of this motivational situation and to describe and analyse it, even though it has not actually been concretely part of the conscious "intention" of the actor; possibly not at all, at least not fully.[10]

We are all familiar with this issue in our own lives. Often we are confused or upset about something that happened to us and about why we reacted as we did. So we turn to others—a close friend, perhaps a family member, maybe a stranger on the bus whom we have never met before and are unlikely to ever meet again. We describe the situation, our feelings, and what we did. And we listen, sometimes gratefully and sometimes with annoyance, as those we turned to give their impressions from the perspective of someone on the outside. Even if we are initially upset by their words, we often come in time to see something in the situation that we had not been able to see before and could not have explained on our own.

This seems an excellent way to describe the social role of the social scientist: That good friend who is willing to tell you something you might not want to hear, and that you come to agree is probably at least largely right.

The Three Voices of Research

But there is a significant complication to Weber's distinction between subjective and explanatory explanations. Not only can the social actor offer some helpful explanatory understanding. The social scientist cannot escape his or her own subjective understanding, sometimes very unhelpfully. If subjective understanding is routinely mixed with explanatory understanding, then explanatory understanding must also be routinely mixed with subjective understanding.

It used to be argued that, with special methodological tools, social scientists could keep their own subjective understandings from polluting their reporting of the subjective understandings of others and from polluting the explanatory understandings they proposed. Hardly anyone in the social sciences believes that any more. For some, our inevitable subjectivity is a cause for despair and doubt about the project of social science, leading to desperate attempts to double-down efforts to become "objective." But for many in qualitative fieldwork, our inevitable subjectivity is, properly understood, the basis for methodological insight and innovation, and thus a cause for celebration. Conducted appropriately and considered thoughtfully, the researcher's subjectivity can indeed be helpful—even necessary.

We will have much more to say about how our bias can be helpful later in the book when we distinguish between "negative bias" (bias that confounds our work) and "positive bias" (bias that makes our work possible). For now, the important point is to recognize that our woes begin when we try to make our work what it is not—and what it cannot be—through some kind of false purity of methodology. In academic debates, we so often find our conversations heading toward the poles of absolutism, as we attempt to impose a single logic on our research. But as with any social situation, research too has many logics—logics that interplay when we gather evidence, when we write, and when our work is read. Research is strongest when it pays attention to its many logics, not when it ignores or attempts to silence them.

In order to help us pay attention to these multiple logics, in this book we describe fieldwork methods as a dialogue between ***three voices of research.*** We refer to the three as the *They*, *You*, and *We* of research. The They voice is the community or group of people who participate in the study. The You voice is the researcher or researchers. And the We voice is the audience or

audiences for the work. All three of these persons (and any one individual may partake of all three of these persons) bring different logics to what the work can and should be. Opposite is a graphic illustration of how the three voices interrelate, including six terms—**multiplicity**, **singularity**, **positionality**, **narrativity**, **contestability**, and **extendability**—that we will introduce in the next three chapters.

Much social science does not recognize (or, perhaps better put, does not admit) how this interplay of logics shapes the scholarly endeavor. The traditional positivism of modernism obscures the researcher and focuses on the They voice of research, extracting information from participants for the academic's gain. The postmodern response has sometimes been to turn inward and focus on the You voice of research, despairing of the ability to learn anything other than a situated knowledge of oneself. And both the modernist and postmodernist at times seem to fear the We voice of the audience as a scowling adversary, not a friendly collaborator. The multilogical approach is a kind of middle way, neither modernist nor postmodernist, neither positivist nor negativist. Rather, it draws on the strengths of both these modes of research and seeks to bring the They and the You into a fuller engagement with the We.

A Cooking Book for Qualitative Fieldwork

We offer this book in the spirit of a multilogical middle way in another sense as well. Books on qualitative research generally follow one of two tacks: "how-to" or "why-to." How-to books take a cookbook approach, offering routines for the safe and sound conduct of qualitative research, sometimes covering a wide gamut of methods and sometimes focusing on one alone. There are literally hundreds of such books available. A few are encyclopedic—the sort of methodological equivalent of *Joy of Cooking* or *Fanny Farmer*, heavy and thick, with a bit of everything.[11] Others offer a single, special style of method, such as focus groups or participant observation—the methodological equivalent of a book on French cooking, say, or vegetarian cooking.[12]

While of great practical value, how-to books tend to sacrifice attention to the intellectual roots of methods, apart from the basic knowledge that is required to carry out a recipe to successful completion. But many qualitative research projects depend upon unusual ingredients and surprising circumstances that do not fit easily with what recipe approaches assume will be in the kitchen of context. In these circumstances—and to some extent all qualitative research will be an imperfect fit with any defined method, to the extent that the research project is new scholarship—a how-to guide can lead the researcher into difficulty.

Some authors have recognized this general problem and responded by offering the second approach: why-to books. This less numerous category focuses on qualitative kitchen craft rather than recipes, methodology rather than methods, philosophy more than technique, theory more than practice. These authors do have practical intent, however. They hope to give researchers the intellectual subtlety to adapt and innovate successfully in the face of circumstances that are new to research. Their emphasis is on problem-solving rather than problem-preventing.[13]

We propose a middle way—a book that offers both methods and methodology, both recipes and general kitchen craft, with a focus on a popular style of qualitative research: fieldwork.[14] It's nice to have some routines that we don't have to think much about, which then allow us to think more carefully about other matters. But when routines don't fit our circumstances—when the ingredients in the recipe can't be found in our cupboards—it's good to have the skills to come up with something else, especially when company is coming and there's no time to shop for the ideal. We call it not a cookbook approach but a *cooking book* approach to qualitative fieldwork.

As with any successful narrative, cooking well requires attention to the They, You, and We of context. The good cook looks at the ingredients that he or she has and cooks with those (the research participants; the They voice). The good cook thinks about what dishes he or she likes to make and what he or she hopes to achieve (the research practitioner; the You voice). The good cook thinks about who is going to be eating the dish and considers their palates and nutritional needs (the research audience; the We voice). So, in thinking about the ingredients of evidence, consider what you have or can get. Don't try to cook something that requires what you don't have or ignores what you do have. In thinking about the cook as a central person, consider how cooking can be something you love—not a chore or an imposition or a frustration—and how doing what you love can lead to better results. In thinking about the audience, think about the cultures of qualitative cuisine (the palate part) and about the usefulness of qualitative work (the nutritional part). It is also good to think about how overtly political a work the audience can tolerate—what we might consider the "spiciness" of the qualitative dish.

However, there is an important caveat to thinking about qualitative fieldwork as cooking: the ingredients in qualitative fieldwork are people. We are tasting lives, consuming people in a way. Soylent Green isn't plankton; it's people! The ethical implications of qualitative fieldwork should be central to its practice. Moreover, unlike cannibalism, the ingredients of this cookery can, and probably will, taste the results. They will taste themselves. What qualitative fieldwork cooks up has practical consequences for our lives. Some of the research participants will likely read what gets written, and some of the people whose actions shape their lives will likely read it too—or be influenced by those who have. Research has implications. Indeed, we hope that it does. Otherwise, why do it? What implications, for whom, and how, all raise issues we will be keeping front and center in this qualitative cooking book.

Another way to think about the ethical issues of real people being ingredients for qualitative cooking is that They are also We. The research participants are also part of the research audience. And, in a sense, the research audience is part of the research participants in that the results of any work of social science may have implications for all of our lives.

They can also be the You voice, or a part of the You voice. A host of new approaches to fieldwork take seriously the value of participatory methods in which the participants may be researchers and the researchers may be participants. Methods like participatory action research, community-based research, auto-ethnography, and performative ethnography have emerged strongly in the last twenty years, as social science has taken up the challenge of understanding how to make bias positive, drawing on the strengths of both subjective and explanatory understanding.

This blending of voices and position in research encourages scholars to consider the broader implications of methodological cooking. Cooking is a political act, the food activists tell us. And they are right. So too with your research. It has consequences outside the kitchen. We wouldn't want it any other way, if our work is to have value. Moreover, what goes on inside the kitchen has an important politics of its own.

Discussions about the ethics and politics of scholarly work can get abstract and theoretical very fast, however. So it is important that we strike a balance with the mundane techniques for how to get the work done and how to put a healthy and safe qualitative dish on the table of scholarship. We say "healthy and safe" to highlight the importance of methods which are at least reasonably "clean" and "sanitary." Past experience has alerted generations of researchers to what we might term "qualitative best practices" or "qualitative hygiene," so that we gather and handle evidence appropriately and what we cook up doesn't make anyone sick—not even the researchers.

In short, with this qualitative cooking book, we hope to join with those works that seek to bridge the old dualism of practice versus theory. Good field research plainly needs them both. We can state the tension as an aphorism: Only a fool would attempt practice without theory, and only a charlatan would attempt theory without practice.

The Form of the Book

We have tried to take account of all of the above in designing the form of the book, reflecting and integrating its many logics.

With that goal in mind, the book takes the reader through the three voices of research in turn. In the next three chapters, we start with the You voice, focusing on the epistemological issues that you as a researcher must consider in conducting multilogical qualitative research. We call this section "Ways of Relating," and each chapter in turn gives a more detailed account of the They, You, and We voices, exploring their relationships to contextuality and intercontextuality.

We turn next to the They voice, discussing the main modes of collecting and analyzing fieldwork evidence. We call this section "Ways of Gathering," and offer three more chapters, one each on "Listening," "Looking," and "Participating." These chapters take the reader through a wide range of fieldwork methods, but not with the encyclopedic coverage of a *Joy of Qualitative Cooking* or the detail of a, say, *When French Women Cook Qualitative*. Still, we have some fun, and hope to offer some clarity, by organizing these chapters as a kind of cooking book, offering both general guidance on why-to and specific recipes of how-to.

Lastly, we discuss the We voice, attending to the writing and the audience of research. We call this section "Ways of Telling," with a chapter each on "The Multilogics of Writing" and "The Promise of Field Work." These chapters also mix why-to and how-to, the intellectual background and recipes for doing—a middle way of qualitative fieldwork and its many logics.

Not all cooks enjoy every part of the kitchen, but that is why we have each other in an entire culinary community. While you might find the philosophy of "Ways of Relating" tiresome, learning how to situate your work in "Way of Telling" might be more up your alley. We present each of the sections for your consideration when your project most needs to hear about that phase of research. Don't get bogged down. Skip around. We certainly did.

The book is multilogical in another sense as well, via its co-authors. Our writing has been a multilogical enterprise. Jason and Mike are different people, of course, and we have tried to draw productively on those differences in the book we have cooked up. Perhaps too many cooks spoils the broth, but two cooks can often work very well together. At least, we have found it so. Yet, as we are different chefs, the book we present here is bit of culinary fusion. Jason's cuisine focuses on the intertwining of race, gender, and sexuality. Mike's dishes tend to focus on the environment, agriculture, and inequality. While Jason works in urban contexts, Mike favors rural ones. To date, Jason's work has been entirely within the US and Mike's projects have ranged from the US to Europe to Africa. Hopefully, such a fusion will provide enough variety of examples to whet anyone's appetite. We encourage you to adjust our recipes for qualitative cookery and even dispute their premises, using your own reasoned reactions to context. Doing so only adds to the multilogical character of the book, of qualitative fieldwork, and of your own research.

Ways of Relating

only at the responses of gay men, not lesbian women or bisexuals. However
nge of audiences that they would be coming out to and the various meanin
o that range. By doing so, his participants were able to tell him someth
different ways to come out and they chose different strategies depend

What about the topic of coming out was Jason interested in? Jason could look at coming out to families, coming out to friends,
coming out to co-workers. He could look at gay men coming out, lesbian women coming out, bisexual men coming out. What did
he even mean by coming out? He could look at what gay men thought coming out was. He could look at media depictions of
coming out to

exists. Whose perspectives should Jason be interested in that situation, men or their mothers? He could study the plans of ga
men. He could look at the memories of the mothers of their reactions to being told their sons were gay. He could interview
who know the men and the mothers to get their recollections of what the men or the mothers may have confided in them
event. Multiplicity goes even further, though. A single perspective on this situation – the gay men's plans to come out

2
THE *THEY* VOICE
Participants and Communities

Of the three voices to consider in conducting any fieldwork project, we take up first the one that is most classically associated with research. The *They* voice refers to those whom you are studying, the group that you are looking at in the situation you will be considering.

Of course, the they-ness of the They voice is relative. Certainly, you will share in some of the concerns of the lives of those whom you are studying, given the commonalities of any human life. A number of methodological issues follow from these commonalities, which we will take up later. But let's consider first two basic decisions that a qualitative fieldworker has to make. Which aspects of the situation you study should you concentrate on? If the situation is sufficiently complex for scholars not to already have a good handle on it, there are likely to be a great many aspects involved. And which people in the situation you study should you include? If the situation is broadly relevant enough to be worth researching, there are likely to be a great many people who at least partially share in that situation and its concerns.

We refer to these companion puzzles of qualitative fieldwork as the problems of *multiplicity* and *singularity*.

Multiplicity

Multiplicity refers to the multiple perspectives and experiences that constitute the context of any social situation. If a situation is social, more than one person is involved. But we never experience a situation in exactly the same way as another because of our different positions, however slight, in the encounter.

So any one situation is as plural as the people in it. And more. Any one situation not only has multiple people in it but also more than one social dynamic at work, from issues of power to patterns of language to routines of self presentation to the range of goals that each person has, and on and on and on. In this sense, any one context is actually multiple contexts—an ever-changing "ecology of contexts," as Mike and his colleague Bill Bland have described elsewhere.[1] And more. Each person in the social situation will have at least a slightly different perspective on, and experience of, those multiple contexts. So multiplicity is multiples of multiples: Multiple people, multiple contexts, multiple perspectives and experiences for each context of the context.

Whew! So multiplicity demands that we answer this question: How will you decide which of the endless multitude of aspects of a social situation are relevant to your concerns?

Let's consider a social situation, one from the very beginning of Jason's research career (when he wasn't even sure that he was going to have one). He was a junior at the University of Texas at Austin at the time, and had just started an honors thesis. Or at least he was thinking about one. On the advice of his academic advisor, he approached Professor Gloria Gonzales-Lopez, who was teaching one of his sociology classes, "Chicana/Latina Sexuality." Showing up at office hours, he told her that he was interested in writing an honors thesis on coming out.

"What about it?" she responded.

A simple but wise and practical question. One thing is always many things. What aspect of the topic of coming out was Jason interested in? Jason could look at coming out to families, coming out to friends, coming out to co-workers. He could look at gay men coming out, lesbian women coming out, bisexual men coming out. What did he even mean by "coming out"? He could look at what gay men thought coming out was. He could look at media depictions of situations of coming out.

In even just one of these situations—for example, gay men coming out to their mothers—multiplicity exists. Whose perspectives should Jason be interested in in that situation, the men or their mothers? He could study the plans of the gay men. He could look at the memories of the mothers of their reactions to being told their sons were gay. He could interview those who knew the men and the mothers to get their recollections of what the men or the mothers may have confided in them about the event (a method called "**triangulation**" that we will discuss in more detail in a subsequent chapter).

Multiplicity goes even further, though. A single perspective on this situation—the gay men's plans to come out to their moms, for example—has multiple other contexts influencing it. Do they have a good relationship with each other? Are they close? Do they live together? What previous experience does the man have with coming out to others? How do media depictions the men have seen have influence their plans? What about the effects of demographic factors like age, race, or income?

When picking any topic, you have to think carefully about these many manynesses. "Everything is so complex!" you may lament. But that is also what makes it interesting and real. Qualitative field researchers generally proceed by embracing complexity and looking for broader significance through the different implications any factor has in social life, not through similarity alone. And fear not: There are ways to do it.

How, then, do you answer the question of which of the endless multitude of aspects of a social situation are relevant to your concerns? *By having a good technique for theory development.*

What theory does is relate things, people, and situations to each other, and relation is relevance. It's a matter of understanding contextuality, of seeing the interacting contexts that come into and move through a situation, however seamlessly or chaotically.

One great way of seeing contexts coming into and through a situation is to begin with what we know from elsewhere. Traditionally, scholars figure out what they want to ask by looking at the research literature. For instance, when Jason began his study on coming out, he started by reading the research literature on coming out. Sitting in front of a computer, pulling up Google Scholar, and typing in (something like) "coming out" is a common way to start research topics. And it is indeed quite valuable. The scholarly literature has a wealth of knowledge related to most any topic. After all, we scholars have been at it for a while already. Plus any scholar has the experience of her own life to draw upon—experience that has to handled with care, to be sure, just like everything else in scholarship.

Thus, a researcher already has considerable knowledge about a topic before she ever sits down to develop her first interview questions. But we need to be wary. Our preconceived notions of the situation and the predefined set of "official" cases from the literature help us see but also blind us. We need pre-existing categories to understand whether what we are seeing fits what we think we know—and thus also whether it does not fit. But it is all too easy to ignore what doesn't fit as we seek a sense of order. We have to have a way to break out of our molds and consider other possible aspects of the situation—its multiplicity—that might have an effect.

The way (or, really, the ways) that qualitative field researchers generally take is to focus on what doesn't fit as much as on what does. You can think of it as being open to multiplicity but from a starting point. In a way, it's a matter of giving space for the They voice, in all its many-ness, to help guide your work, as an active agent within the research process.

Two common methods of theory development in qualitative methods are *extended case method* (ECM), popularized by Michael Burawoy (1998), and *grounded theory* (GT), first developed by Glaser and Strauss (1967). ECM develops theory by starting with a general account of the world and then selecting a case that will extend that theory to new situations, changing it in the process to handle differences brought up by the new case. It's the more deductive approach of the two. GT takes the opposite route to the same destination. GT starts with a particular situation and then branches outwards to develop a theory that can explain other cases. It's the more inductive approach.

Both ECM and GT consider multiplicity, but from different angles.[2] ECM engages with multiplicity by considering the many different contexts that a theory applies to before drilling down into a particular one. GT moves the other way by thinking about all the contexts that influence the one case. It has participants guide the researcher to some of the most interesting instances and situations.

Having a qualitative tradition and direction helps many researchers, so pick one. Our guess is that you will rapidly find that you start moving in the other direction at least a bit as well. In practice, ECM often morphs into GT, and vice versa. We regard these two approaches more as starting points in an endless circle of deduction and induction. But you need a direction to begin with. Are you pretty sure in advance you know what theoretical debate you hope to contribute to? Go with ECM. Not sure? Go with GT. Regardless of the direction—deductive or inductive—both

ECM and GT encourage us to consider new situations in all their multiplicity, developing our theory and focusing our eye, while letting the They voice into our research to confound, surprise, and ultimately educate us.

Singularity

But it isn't possible to study it all. Singularity refers to the difference that is inherent with any situation in, perspective on, and experience of the contexts of social life. While multiplicity urges us to think about the manyness of every situation, perspective, and experience, singularity reminds us that every situation, perspective, and experience is also at least a little bit unique. Each case has its own combination of people and factors and thus a somewhat different logic to its workings. Never—when we see a situation, interview a person, observe a scene, or read an article—do we experience an exact repeat of any combination. Assuredly, we will see social factors that influence more than one case, if it is indeed a social factor. And what we see in any one case is never completly isolated, or we could not have seen that case. (If something is completely isolated, you can't ever see it, or even know it.) What we do see is contexts intercontextually shaping other contexts. But how it works out in any one instance is never an exact repeat.

At first consideration, singularity may seem a maddening problem for the qualitative researcher—as maddening as multiplicity. Returning to Jason's senior honors thesis, when Dr. Gonzalez-Lopez asked him, "What about it?" she was not only invoking multiplicity, but drawing him to singularity. She was also asking him to appreciate difference as much as the similarity we often think it is the task of the scholar to uncover, in order to make a generalization. Consider research Mike is currently conducting among the amaQwathi people of South Africa's Eastern Cape Province. To the outsider, the amaQwathi seem much like the amaXhosa, a much larger group, even speaking the same language. But they have a distinct history and situation. Moreover, the social dynamics of personalities, the possibilities of the landscape, and the ambitions people have for their lives differ within each amaQwathi village, sometimes markedly so—even though they are all amaQwathi.

Think of it this way. Multiplicity focuses us on aspects. Singularity focuses us on instances. Out of the huge population that he could potentially study, and their many situations, whom and which should he investigate? Everyone and every moment is assuredly a little bit different, so a complete study would indeed cover every single, singular one. But it would have been impossible for Jason to study every instance in every situation. While it is vital to consider the singularity of the situation, there are both practical and theoretical limitations.

Practically, no matter the size of the research team, even if you have a million-dollar National Institute of Health grant, one cannot observe everything. There will always be something missing. The contextuality and intercontexuality of any situation makes collecting data on everything impossible.

If one wants to make an intervention in research literature, then one cannot speak to everything at once. Journal articles and books make limited claims. They speak to particular audiences about specific research questions. A research project that considers too much will not be able to talk about the question with enough specificity to convince scholars that one has considered the situation in enough depth.

So singularity demands that a researcher answer this question: How will you account for whom and where you research and, more importantly, whom and where you do not? If practically and theoretically we cannot study everything, then we need to not only pick a topic, we must be able to justify what we left out. Every situation is unique. So why did the researcher pick these specific cases?

In Jason's example, he chose to look at the responses of gay men, not lesbian women or bisexuals. However, he kept open the range of audiences that they would be coming out to and the various meanings that coming out had to that range. By doing so, his participants were able to tell him something new: there were a lot of different ways to come out and they chose different strategies depending on the audience that they were coming out to.

His decision to only look at gay men came out of the research literature. Previous work claimed that gay men, lesbian women, and bisexuals came out differently. Since he wanted to determine how the audience influenced how they came out, it was sufficient to emphasize the diversity of the audience. In doing so, however, he was accepting the helpfulness of a category widely used by the research literature as well as in popular culture: a category of person we may call "gay men." A moment's reflection on the multiplicity of social life will yield the recognition that there is a lot of diversity within the category "gay men," which Jason's work did not emphasize. Which is fine—indeed, it is often necessary. We need categories to establish relationships, differences to establish connections. Otherwise there would be nothing to relate and connect. We need what some scholars call "strategic essentialism," not only to change the world but also to describe it (the latter being necessary for any deliberate change).[3] And we need in a subsequent phase of action and scholarship to look at the diversity within the categories we just used—for which we will need more categories, more strategic essentialism, in order to envision that diversity. Indeed, in Jason's current ethnographic work, a central focus is looking within the category "gay men."

To use and construct categories that limit the diversity of the social is necessarily to tell a story, just as it is necessary for telling a story. You can't ever present all of reality. It is too multiple in all its infinite singularity. Instead, you have to represent it. You have to have a narrative—a point we will consider in more detail later. The philosophical problem here is inescapable.

But as with so many problems, the first step to solving it is accepting it. How will you account for whom and where you research and whom and where you do not? *By developing a strong* **population narrative** *with a compelling point of contrast or path of social action to follow and investigate.*

By "population narrative," we mean an account of why, for the problem you seek to investigate, it makes sense to focus on the people and situations that you studied and not on those you didn't study. And there is nothing to be embarrassed about here in seeing this account as a narrative, a story we tell—as long we do not pretend that the categories we use to develop our population narrative are permanent and inviolable. Rather, it is necessary for research to be able to define what we are looking at, or we won't be able to see it at all. And that means having a point of contrast, or a path of social action, that allows us to distinguish something out of the flickering shadows into which we peer, and gives our research something to account for, some difference to explain or upon which to construct an explanation. In Jason's study, his population narrative constrained a particular contrast—sexual identity—and introduced variation in another contrast—audience. But he did this constraining strategically, recognizing that other research could usefully open up what he limited.

In this way, a population narrative guides the qualitative researcher in working through two traditional questions in research concerning the They voice: sampling and recruitment. But multilogical approaches to qualitative research handle these questions with important differences. In positivistic science, a scholar settles on They before going out into the field. You think about the population that you are interested in and decide on the sample you need to draw from that population to be able to make generalizations about it. You only consider They in terms of the sampling techniques and recruitment strategies you need to gain your sample. Scholars in this mode of science do not think about the people they study as participants in the research but as a pool of cases from which to extract data. In this sense, They becomes Them.

In multilogical research, though, the people we study are far more than a sample. They are involved in the production of the research questions, analysis, and final product. Their logic becomes one of the multiple logics embodied in the research. In some approaches, those we study are involved directly through actually helping guide and conduct the research (as we will talk about in more detail in chapter 7, which focuses on participatory research). The They, You, and We voices of research merge. We all become We. For example, in Mike's work among the amaQwathi, the villagers participate with the outside researchers in setting research priorities, gathering evidence, and interpreting the results, ensuring accuracy and practical relevance.

In addition, the They voice also indirectly shapes the study by clueing researchers into the complexity of the situation and its specificity, the ways in which it is unique from other situations. As field researchers become better informed, their research questions develop. And as the questions develop, so too does the researcher's sense of the people and situations that are most relevant to study. By constantly re-evaluating whom we should study, in step with what we are learning from them in the field, our sense of the logics involved in the research setting becomes ever more multiple. In short, in multilogical work, sampling and recruitment change as the work proceeds.

Does this mean that the multilogical sample is not representative? In most multilogical research, no, it is not representative. Rather, the sample is openly singular. But a lack of representativeness is not necessarily a problem for research—as long as we know the contextuality of the sample, and thus its degrees of intercontextuality. The cogency of the work rests not on whether or not the sample is representative, but rather on our understanding of what is present in the case. We call this the *presentedness* of the case, our understanding of the contextuality and intercontextually that are present in it. In Jason's study of coming out, he looked at the ways the audience changed the context in which the men came out and thus how they did it. Jason did not, however, study the entire range of possible audiences. That would not have been possible. But the singular situations he did study were located in an ecology of contexts that extends as **inter-contexts** into other singular situations, in varying combinations. No doubt the way gay men come out in those other situations will, well, come out differently—but for reasons scholars can better appreciate because of what Jason saw elsewhere.

Thus, from a knowledge of contextuality, we are able to use a sample intercontextually, connecting the multiplicity of the settings of our research with other social settings whose contextuality we also understand, in all their multilogical singularity.

RECIPES FOR THE *THEY* VOICE

1. A CONTEXT DUMP

In some productivity systems, like Getting Things Done (GTD), they ask you to start your week off with a "brain dump" of everything you need to accomplish. Writing down everything one needs to do can actually be very difficult, so "trigger lists" were developed to help people remember tasks. In this spirit, we offer the trigger list below. This exercise in multiplicity will help you generate many different possible contextual influences. It isn't meant to be an exhaustive list of all possible contexts. Add anything you can think of. We'll use this mind map in the next recipe on singularity.

Take a large sheet of paper or mind-mapping software and write your project idea or topic in the center. Draw a circle around it.

Everywhere else on the page, wherever feels natural, write down the different contextual influences in your project. Use the trigger list below to help kick-start your brain. For each one, ask yourself: " What context in my project does the word evoke? What contrast does the word inspire me to explore?"

Identities:

- Race
- Ethnicities
- Gender
- Sexuality
- Ability
- Disability
- Class Position
- Rural/Urban
- Religious Participation
- Occupation
- Social Roles
- Family Roles
- Marital Status
- Lifespan/Life Course
- Development
- Age
- Citizenship
- Physical Health
- Mental Health

Structural:

- Place and Space
- Governmental Systems
- Penal justice system
- Economic Systems
- History
- Foreign/Occupations
- Colonial/Postcolonial
- Residential Segregation/ Integration
- Educational Systems
- Immigration/Migration
- Roads and Transportation
- Ecology
- Resources
- Climate

Cultural:

- Mass Media
- Independent Media
- Social Media
- Political Parties
- Science
- Religion
- Academia
- Technology
- Language
- Foodways
- Cultural Capital

Communities:

- Political Organizations
- Businesses
- Non-governmental Organizations
- Places of worship
- Schools
- Community Centers
- Nightclubs/Bars
- Restaurants
- Parks
- Neighborhoods
- Public Transit

- Public Assistance
- Institutions
- Social Capital

Micro/Interactional:

- Conversational Rules
- Ethnomethodology
- Presentation of Self
- Agency
- Time
- Perception
- Cognition
- Biology/Genetics/Evolution
- Embodiment
- Group Structure/Group
- Cohesion/Groupthink
- Intergroup Conflict
- Social Support
- Socialization
- Attraction
- Emotions
- Rationality

2. Population Narratives

It's impossible to do it all. Frankly, it's not all interesting or worth exploring anyways. We have precious research time, money, and other resources that we have to devote to only the most important questions. Thus, it's important that we develop a population narrative that can help us define the point of contrast we should study. In this exercise, we use the contextual influences we generated through exploring our topic's multiplicity to cut down to the essential.

First, take the map of contextual influences and select three. One should be the context that jumps out at you intuitively as the most important. One should be an influence that the community of scholars or your audience would consider important to include. One should be compelling or practically interesting to a population you are considering studying.

Second, for each of these contexts, we need to generate a set of cases that will help us learn about that perspective. Brainstorm some specific singular communities, the "They". Who would you study to learn about that context? For example, don't just list farmers if you're interested in sustainable agriculture. Instead, get specific: rural farmers in X County in Iowa.

Third, a population narrative isn't simply the population you will study. It includes the point of contrast or social path that will make your study compelling. Look at the contexts and cases you generated. How can you combine them and contrast them to define a population narrative? In our example, if social class led us to consider farm size as well as the farmers in X County in Iowa, then a population narrative would mean studying large and small farms in X County. An additional point of contrast might be to study both large and small conventional as well as sustainable farms in X County. The singularity of these cases will help to make our work both contestable and extendable, to make your work generalizable by being as specific as possible.

3. Link Holes and "The Literature"

It's easy to lose yourself on Wikipedia. While writing an email to a friend about moving, you look up the population of Toronto. Then, you enter a time warp. An hour later, you realize that your browser is flooded with tabs to Wikipedia articles. You've fallen down a link hole. Clicking from article to article, you found a multiplicity of contexts that relate to your original question. Not all of them were relevant, but many were interesting, leading you further down. After all, within 4 clicks of Toronto on Wikipedia is as diverse information as the Haldimand Proclamation, a British decree giving land to the Iroquois after the American Revolution, and Pop Art, a 1950s art movement focusing on taking popular culture images out of context.

"The Literature" often looms large. Many see it simultaneously as a trove of academic experience and a tomb of secrets, a paper waiting just out of sight that will "scoop" your topic. Because the literature seems unmanageable, people tend to stick to their subfields, selecting ever narrower interests within the delimited area that they've become experts in.

However, it is easy to get a handle on new topics through the link hole method. By quickly coming up to speed on a new contextual factor, we are better able to respond to the multiplicity of our case. Traditional methods of searching the literature—abstracting databases and search engines—focus overly on recent articles, giving a broad view of recent developments, but it can be hard to triangulate on key concepts in a new area.

Start with an article on your topic, preferably one that appeared in the pages of your discipline's top journals within the last few years. Reading, find three references that seem even more relevant to your research question. Within those articles, do the same, finding three references. Doing so again will net a total of 40 articles. Likely, you'll have noticed that many of these articles cite each other. 40 articles isn't everything, but it is a manageable microcosm of multiplicity.

4. The Trouble with Categories

Without categories—identities, groups, labels, etc.—studying the social would be impossible. We have to group people together to understand their similarities and differences. However, within any category is the endless confusing multiplicity and singularity that leads us to often lament their uselessness.

Intersectionality, the feminist philosophical and methodological movement, studies the overlapping and intersections between social categories. Leslie McCall[4] developed a useful typology for intersectionality that we can use for our own studies to ensure we are not merely repeating taken-for-granted categories or ignoring their usefulness.

Anticategorical complexity refers to the diversity within any category. These studies tend to break apart and critique a category, demonstrating the variation within it. For instance, Rogers Brubaker[5] showed that some groups, like residents of a nation, should not be treated as such analytically, because they do not see themselves as such and don't act as though they were grouped.

Intracategorical complexity looks at unexamined intersections between categories and is the kind of study most often associated with intersectionality. How are the experiences of black lesbians different from white lesbians, black gay men, or heterosexual black women? How does their black identity and lesbian identity interact to make both experiences different? Mignon Moore's book *Invisible Families*[6] uses intracategorical complexity to examine these issues.

Intercategorical complexity is at the other end, using strategic essentialism to examine and compare between groups as though they were internally consistent. These studies are different to traditional uses of groups in the acknowledgment that the categories are unstable and often conflicting. For instance, Jason's study of coming out[7] in gay men uses the category of "gay," although much research suggests that there is exceptional diversity of sexual orientations within this category. However, people treat it as a group, and learning about their experiences led him to expand our understanding of how people tell others stigmatizing information.

Consider each kind of intersectionality, even if one doesn't draw upon intersectionality as an area in your work, as a question for our work. These questions can potentially lead to research questions or help us define our population narrative. Break open categories, compare them, and strategically accept their use.

opening up the curtain of your story and making your narrativity visible

3
THE *YOU* VOICE
Researchers

You are the researcher. As such, your voice will always be present in the project. We are often encouraged to think of research as figuring out the unbiased truth of a question from a population. However, you are an important part of the research because you are the person, or one of the people, asking the questions, as well as the person analyzing the data and developing it into a narrative that will be presented to others. And that is not necessarily a bad thing. But we have to consider the ways in which you will be affecting the research and how you, or you and your research colleagues, can present those decisions within the research. We have to consider the place of the You voice in the multilogical dialogue of research.

Traditionally, there have been two different extremes in dealing with the researcher's role. The positivist position is that the researcher is at best a necessary evil. Positivism wants to silence the You voice, attempting to get rid of it entirely, if possible. It's as though the researcher were only a tool, a drill to extract information from They for use by We, the audience for research we will discuss in the next chapter. This approach is epitomized by the ideal of replication: reliable research as a formula that can be carried out by any trained person, with the same inevitable result. Anyone who follows the exact same steps will discover the exact same information about the exact same research question.

Postmodern scholarship argued that replication was not possible, and was more of a ritual than a virtue. Any two researchers are each going to find something slightly different because they have different ways of responding to the project, and because those we study will respond differently to the researchers. It is a Sisyphean task to try and make everything exactly the same. Moreover, the closer we come to replication, the less interesting we make our work. And the less realistic: We achieve replication by narrowing our vision so much that we don't appreciate the conflicts and mess that lie just outside our field of view. One huge source of that conflict and mess is the researcher herself/himself, with all her or his biases and agendas. Postmodernism, though, sometimes goes to the other extreme. Some moods within postmodernism encourage us to believe that, because we are all biased, there is no way for us to really know anything about anyone, except maybe for ourselves—with an emphasis on "maybe" even there. Such an extreme postmodern approach silences the They voice, focusing on studying and interpreting the You.

In this book, we encourage you to take a middle way here as well. Consider the You voice as a facilitator between They and We. To achieve that facilitation, you have to be upfront about the ways in which the field researcher affects the research being produced. Absolute replication is impossible. However, it is still possible for us to know things about others. And you, the field researcher, can be a conduit through which community understandings enter into dialogue with the wider communities of scholarship and the public at large, making it possible for even more of us to know even more about, well, even more of us.

There are two aspects of You that we need to understand to properly consider the researcher's role in producing field research. We need to consider the ways the researcher's own identities and relationships to society will affect the research produced. We also need to think about how and why you decide what to tell people about what other people said and did, and not have field research be just a highfalutin' form of gossip. These two aspects are *positionality* and *narrativity*.

Positionality

Positionality refers to the researcher's own location in social life, with all the partiality of vision and political commitment that comes with anyone's social location. The postmodernists are surely right in their view that researchers are as sociological as anyone else. In a way, positivism makes the same point, although it holds that proper method can overcome the problem and remove the researcher's own sociology from the results. Few in the social sciences today believe this removal is fully possible. Nevertheless, many still contend that we can come close. And the debate rages on.

Whether or not it is possible to come close to removing the You, with a multilogical approach it is neither necessary nor desirable, as we will explore. But it is definitely necessary to address the research challenge raised by positionality: How will you account for your role in co-generating the data that you are going to analyze? By distinguishing between the negative and positive influences that your positionality has on your research.

Because you choose the questions that you ask—albeit possibly in conjunction with others (including the They, if the work is participatory). You choose the places that you go to make your observations and the people that you talk to. In the language of Grounded Theory, you have pre-existing "sensitizing concepts" which lead you to make certain decisions in the research process. The data that you collect will always be partial because your positioning makes it hard for you to see some of the things going on in the contexts you are researching. You can't analyze what you don't even think to collect.

Relatedly, your social position in the field influences the kinds of information you are able to gather—even if your sensitizing concepts have alerted you to seek them. There will always be parts of the context that you are studying which you will not be able to access. There will always be people you won't be able to talk to, possibly because they refuse to talk to someone like you. There could even be places you aren't able—or allowed—to go to. And even in the places you are able to go, people may act differently because of who you are. You are a person, not a secret video camera. (Indeed, in most circumstances it would be unethical to use a secret video camera and research ethics review boards most likely would not allow it.) Besides, even if you did use a secret video camera, no camera can be everywhere. (This is not *The Hunger Games*!) So you are always going to have a partial view. It will be impossible for you to get a complete collection of data free from the influence of who you are and your research process. Someone else coming in will have a different positionality. They will have access to different people. They will think to ask different questions. They will be told different things.

Doesn't this make qualitative research impossibly biased? If you can't guarantee that we will get the full story—collect all the data—then how can we know that you are going to tell us what really happened?

Yes, it is impossible to control yourself as though you were a variable in a linear regression equation or an apparatus in an experiment—even in the most participatory of projects. There will always be some kind of influence of you on the situation. There is a kind of "Heisenberg uncertainty principle" of qualitative research, an "observer effect", just as there is even in physics, as Werner Heisenberg pointed out about quantum mechanics long ago. But rather than seeing this effect as only negative, we want to encourage you to consider how it can also help your research.

You are a multiplicity of contexts embodied in the singularity of a person. You have experiences that others do not have. You also likely have years of training in a discipline, giving you knowledge and connections that others won't have when looking at the same situation. You are a lens that automatically refracts the cases you've chosen. But a lens does more than distort and limit; it can also bring certain elements into sharper focus.

Distinguish between what we call ***negative bias*** and ***positive bias***. Negative bias is bias in the conventional sense: it's the ways in which your positionality distorts your analysis or prevents you from accessing certain aspects of the situation. Negative bias makes you miss some of the multiplicity. It blinds you to the situation's singularity.

Positive bias, though, flips that on its head. Positive bias is the ways your positionality allows you to gain access to certain experiences and social evidence and gives you insight into the situation that others might not have. In these ways, your positionality can be helpful to your research. How? Belonging to a social group or social category, for instance, could help you with access and insight. To paraphrase the sociologist Marjorie Devault, it could help you translate things that are incompletely said, filling in meaning through understanding when someone is not fully articulate.[1] (Indeed, everything is always incompletely said, because of time constraints and the constant unfolding of social life.) Someone less familiar with the situation might misinterpret a phrase or misunderstand an idiom.

Plus, it is not only our social familiarity that gives us insight. Not belonging to a group or category, or not belonging fully, could help you see something that someone else would consider natural to the situation, unquestionable and unremarkable. It sometimes takes ***the stranger*** to interrogate the ordinary, as Georg Simmel, a founding figure of the discipline of sociology, once observed. Indeed, groups implicitly recognize the potential of the stranger's insight. In Simmel's words, the stranger "often receives the most surprising openness—confidences which sometimes have the character of a confessional and which would be carefully withheld from a more closely related person."[2] The stranger could even be considered partially a member of the group, "near and far at the same time," as Simmel put it.[3] For we often value what others who are a bit removed from a situation have to say about it, and even seek them out. In this sense, we could perhaps consider the social researcher a "professional stranger," as Michael Agar has phrased it.[4]

All researchers are going to be biased. Live with it. And think about it. Carefully. But we also ask you to consider how your bias may help your work. Herein lies the solution to the worry that your positionality turns your work into "mere bias." *Think through how to make your biases positive.*

In Jason's first research project, it would not have been right for him to try to ignore the fact that he was a gay man like his participants.[5] Traditionally, researching those with a similar identity to the researcher would likely have been considered bad form: How could he be objective? But because Jason is also gay, there were times when his participants made comments that a straight researcher might not have been able to understand. As Devault comments, there are times when people from minority groups are unable to fully express their experience because the language we use is constructed by the majority.[6] A researcher with similar experience can help "translate" these moments.

But in addition, Jason was a bit of a stranger to his research subjects—and not only because they did not know him personally. As a sociologist, he came to the research with perspectives that were not common among his participants, perspectives drawn from his professional discipline. The dynamics of being a stranger can also go the other way, in potentially equally positive ways: being a stranger to sociology. In Jason's case, this form of positive bias influenced how he chose his research topic in the first place. As a gay man reading the research literature on coming out, he found a number of ways in which the research did not describe his experience or that of his friends. This kind of positionality of being a stranger to the discipline can be a great way to find a research topic. Since context is so important to understanding social life, we can look at the context of our own lives for situations that don't seem to fit with current academic understandings.

As a stranger, people in a fieldwork setting will often consider the researcher as an "interested innocent," who honors them through genuine curiosity about their lives. So they are often quite willing to talk about personal or difficult matters. Take Mike's first research project, researching the relationship between social class and ideas of nature in England. His position as the stranger allowed him to ask many questions that might have been considered rude coming from an English person. Class in England is a very sensitive topic, given the continued strength of the Victorian legacy—in some ways as sensitive as race in the US. Mike could ask about the most basic aspects of these sensitivities because people generally perceived him as not having a stake in it, coming from another country, and especially a country that many in England regard as not having class dynamics.

Of course, the US very much does have class dynamics, and Mike certainly has a class position and many outlooks associated with that position. The potential benefits of positive bias should not lead us to neglect careful consideration of our negative bias. Jason's next research project was on racism in queer communities. Sure, he is gay and sees the racism going on around him in gay-identified spaces he visits. However, he is also white. He has social experiences and social privileges derived from the social construction of race that makes it harder for him to understand and appreciate some aspects of the lives of those of different races, or even to be in a position to see or hear about those aspects. The same goes for Mike, who is also white. Mike and Jason might easily have missed important features of racism in the communities they studied, and they needed to have research strategies to take into account their potential blindnesses. But even with regard to race, one of the social factors that most divides us, there can be a positive dimension to bias. As a white man, Jason had access to people and places that, because of racism, queer people of color would have trouble gaining access to. The same applied to Mike in his work in England and South Africa.

In short, it is important to understand and conduct research from many different positionalities and their standpoints. Recognizing the significance, and potential value, of positionality in research also alerts us to the significance and value of bringing together the multiple logics of our multiple positions.

Narrativity

But any conversation is limited by time and by space. You are almost certain to collect way, way more information in your qualitative research project than you can possibly convey in a scholarly paper or even a book. For his dissertation research on the relationship between social class and ideas of nature in England, which later became a book, Mike conducted 81 hours of recorded interviews. People speak about 100 to 250 words per minute, depending on the dynamics of a conversation. The pace of interviews is usually slow and thoughtful and 125 words a minute is pretty typical. So an hour of interview material usually works out at about 7500 words, or roughly 30 pages of double-spaced transcription. So that means Mike recorded what would have amounted to 2430 pages of interviews—if it had all been transcribed. Mike had fully intended to do so, nobly, but in the end he worked his way through a little less than half of it. Even that 1000 pages of stuff was way, way more than he could have fitted into even a very lengthy dissertation or the 279-page book he eventually published. And that's not even considering his analysis and his reporting of evidence that came from methods other than interviewing, such as observation and historical documents. He estimates that at most a tenth of the material he transcribed wound up in the book—that is, a tenth of the less than half of all his interviews that even got transcribed. So no more than 5 percent of his interview material made it to print.

We hope you will learn from Mike's experience and not attempt 81 hours of recorded interviews! It just isn't practical. Nor is it necessary if you have a good method for theory development and a strong population narrative. But even if you do rein things in to, say, 30 to 40 hours of interviews—a pretty typical figure—you will still have way more interview text than you can include. Even just 10 hours of interview material would likely yield 300 pages of transcripts. You don't have enough space to include all of it.

A conundrum of qualitative research is that it gives you both too much evidence and not enough. As a field researcher, you are close to the social context under study, in all its multiplicity. You are usually very aware, often painfully aware, that you are missing a huge amount about people's lives. So there you go again, getting another five interviews and doing another five hours of participant observation—which only leads you to want another five and another five, and so on. Plus qualitative evidence is very bulky. It doesn't crunch easily into neat categorical piles. It's real-time data. Yes, there are qualitative software packages, and they can help a lot. But you still have to keystroke real-time into words in an electronic file. Too much, and not enough.

So you will have to be selective about what you report. This need to reduce comes on top of the selectiveness, however intentional or unintentional, arising from issues of positionality, which limited the evidence you were able to collect to begin with. And can we complicate the situation even more? You also have to consider not only the time and space limits of your evidence but also the time and space limits of your audience. Its members don't have time to read through all your evidence. You might be frustrated by the 8000-word limit of the typical academic social science journal article, but readers are usually grateful for it.

Plus, you can't write an article or book that will appeal to, or even make sense to, all possible readers. Unless she is a trained social scientist, your mother will likely find tedious a lot of what you want to say to your professional colleagues. Maybe you'd rather write something that would appeal to your mother or to other general readers, but you have professional needs to connect to academic debates. In short, you can't write for all social spaces at once. If your work is to be successful you will have to think about who your audience is and construct your account accordingly. You will have to try to be persuasive and to make a good impression on the audience. That probably means leaving some things out, reporting only certain aspects of what you do include, and using language and organization schemes that deliberately attempt to connect with your intended readers.

What we mean by the term narrativity is that, like it or not, you are a storyteller. Sounds like more bias, and it is. And it raises another set of challenges to the qualitative researcher: How will you justify the inevitable need to select, reduce, and construct a story, which leads to partiality? The answer is closely related to the answer we gave for the problem of positionality: *By opening up the curtain of your story and making your narrativity visible.*

The troubles come when we attempt ***invisible narrativity*** through routines of storytelling that suggest that there is no choice-making author behind the work and that the work is more authoritative because it has no apparent author. Instead, the multilogical researcher embraces the need to make choices, makes them consciously and carefully, and does not attempt to disguise her authorship and disappear, like the Wizard of Oz, behind a curtain that blocks the view of the author. She recognizes that conveying the positionality of the choice-making author is both more methodologically accurate and a way to bring readers into better dialogue with the research participants, for readers can then take the author's positionality into account. Central to knowledge is the position from which we see it—which doesn't necessarily make the knowledge wrong. Rather, knowing that position better enables us to understand how things might look from another angle, another perspective, another logic.

So rather than narrative invisibility, the multilogical researcher strives for ***visible narrativity***, or what we might think of as a kind of "positive narrativity." One immediate warning, though: Although acknowledging positionality is important, you don't want to obscure the social experience of the participants in your research. Your goal is just the opposite: To convey their lives to readers, not your life—except to the extent that conveying your life helps convey theirs. Your singular experience is unlikely to be the reason why someone wants to read and learn from your research. Your positionality matters, but it isn't everything. You want to be a facilitator between They and We, without taking over the conversation. You want to connect context to context through context—We to They via You—and thus build intercontextuality.

Our later chapter on participation describes methods that researchers can use to integrate themselves into their project without it becoming an exercise in narcissism and self-indulgence. The larger point to grasp now, though, is that authorship is authority and authority is authorship. What do we mean by that? Your public presence as an author, sanctioned by a publisher, gives you authority. Plus you only got to be an author because you had a degree of authority to begin with. We are talking about power, the power to write and the power that comes from writing. Thus, the act of writing is also an act of responsibility because the published work has a powerful voice in creating the social world in which people live. Social sciences are unique in that the object of study—society—responds and changes in response to a scientific finding. Conveying the narrativity—the story you are presenting and creating—is an important way to consider, mitigate, and ensure the accountability of that power.

RECIPES FOR THE *YOU* VOICE

1. WHO AM I?

In social psychology, one learns that the self-concept "Who am I?" in our society is often answered categorically. That is to say, it is answered with structural categories that our society provides in identities and roles. In 1954, Manfred Kuhn and Thomas McPartland developed the Twenty Statements Test to help identify the different identities and roles that make up your self-concept.

First, write twenty statements that begin with the phrase, "I am … ."

Next, choose five of these identities and their associated social interests. How will each of them influence your project positively and negatively?

Then, for each of these positive and negative biases, how will your project handle them? How can you minimize the negative bias and maximize the positive bias?

2. THE FAMILIAR STRANGER

We are insiders and outsiders, always. To maximize the benefits of both, you must occupy the liminal space, the threshold between friend and stranger.

To practice, try to look at a place that you go to regularly with fresh eyes, as though you had never seen it. In the study of deviance, this is studied through "breaching" or intentionally acting against the implicit rules of a space to see how people react. Instead of breaking the rules, spend an hour observing a space that you normally attend, like a class, a social event, a meeting, a bar, a church gathering, or a party. What are the rules of this space? Is there a formal way for people to figure out the order of events—are they taught?—or is the training informal? What would happen if someone broke the rules?

3. The Interested Innocent

Conversely, if you are to do qualitative fieldwork, then you will have to get used to the sensation of discomfort that comes from being in an unfamiliar space, not knowing what you are doing, unsure of how your positionality fits with those around you. Becoming the interested innocent with strangers will get easier with practice.

For this exercise, go learn a new skill, sport, craft, or activity. Many cities and towns offer adult education classes, meet-ups, free events, and other ways to plunge yourself into an unfamiliar space in which it is socially expected for you to be inept and ask frequent questions of those experts around you. Pick a skill that you genuinely don't know. You will be surprised at the generosity of those willing to help you learn Ultimate Frisbee or how to fix a bicycle. You might have some fun at it too!

4. Communicating Your Story

Narrativity compels us to consider the ways that we transmit our work as a story, acting as a facilitator between the They and We voices. In this exercise, we ask you to consider how you will discuss your project with different audiences and the methodological choices that result from that choice. If what the project is "about" is different for different audiences and we will discuss it differently in different venues, then we must consider from the beginning how these audiences will shape our work.

How would you explain your project to different audiences? For each of the audiences below, write a few sentences on your project's narrative to this group. Consider each as asking that dreaded question: "So, what are you studying again?" Don't focus on how the work is practically applicable to that group. Instead, how will you describe the methods, topic, and research questions?

Your parents, close relatives, or immediate family
Social Media (Facebook, Twitter, Tumblr, etc). Compose a tweet (140 characters).

Undergraduates at a university or college
Granters, national agencies, or other funding allocators
Your advisor, department chair, tenure committee, or other internal audience
The community or population you're studying (They)
Your discipline as a whole (We)

5. Shining a Light

Narrativity is present in every piece of writing because it is impossible to convey all information available to the audience. That's the point of writers, academics, and journalists, after all! If you wanted to read all of the source material, then you wouldn't have a need for their work. You would just do it yourself.

The problem, of course, is when writers use invisible narrativity, which suggests that there was no choice-making involved in its production—as though "factual reporting" were a matter of bland description and rote observation. This is easiest to spot in the passive writing of natural science, but any discipline's works will usually have authors hiding behind the curtain.

Take an article out of the latest copy of a top journal in your field. Read it with the goal of critiquing its narrativity, using some of the questions below. Notice that these questions also strike at the issue of contestability, the subject of the next chapter.

- Does the author provide an entry trope, or reason for their answering their research question? Or does the author present the research as having sprung fully formed?
- Does the author discuss how they chose which participant's quotes, scenes, or information to present in the text?
- Does the author present their selection biases and recruitment strategy? Or does the author present the participants as passive, just magically showing up at the door?
- Does the author present their analytical strategy and their positional interests?

6. Authorial Authority

The power of the pen. As the person writing, you have the privilege and the responsibility of presenting the information and starting the dialogue on a topic. You're often going to be the first person to bring certain information out into the academic world. Getting it wrong—especially if you get something wrong intentionally—creates a major ethical problem. However, just as serious is putting something down on paper that, while true, shouldn't be presented.

Instructors usually teach this point by looking at massive ethical screw-ups such as Humphrey's Tea Room Trade or other instances where someone has misused their power putting something into words. However, there are many everyday concerns that are closer to home:

- Do you record your participant's criminal activity? If the court compels you to provide your **field notes**, what would they find?
- What about where they live? In an ethnography on immigration, for instance, this information could be used by officers to deport someone.
- What efforts will you take to hide or elude efforts to decode participants? That is, sometimes a pseudonym is not enough to protect someone's confidentiality. Will you name the place in which you worked? Jason, for instance, identifies the neighborhood in Chicago where he worked, but Mike hides the name of the village in England with the pseudonym "Childerley."

These kinds of questions go beyond what is usually required by an Institutional Review Board or standard consent form. Don't give it minimum ethical thought. Think it through.

© Matt Raboin

4
THE *WE* VOICE
The Audience

The least discussed voice in research is We, the community of scholars and the general public who will read your research. You've thought about the multiplicity of the context and constrained it in some way to enjoy and learn from its singularity. You've selected and conducted your research based on your positionality, and you're consciously and openly going to present it as a narrative. Now you have to make it more than "just your interpretation." You have to convince readers that your work is reputable and worthwhile. You have to give them the tools to dispute with you and to make your work applicable to other contexts. You have to consider your work's *contestability* and *extendability*, and you have to answer the questions that each demands: How will you challenge your interpretations and make them scientific, and how will you make the case that your research is broadly significant and worth paying attention to?

Contestability

"Mr. Bell, can you tell us in what way your work differs from fiction?" That troublesome question from chapter 1 again.

The question of fiction pertains to our evaluation of all scientific work. But because of the cultural history of scientific endeavor, it is a challenge more often raised about qualitative work, especially qualitative fieldwork. The researcher is the data collection instrument in qualitative fieldwork. Every such instrument is as different from others as one researcher is from another. So qualitative data cannot be (or at least should not be) separated from the researcher, raising the specter of manipulation for a desired result and the concern that another data collection instrument might have registered something different. The You voice transmits the They voice to the We voice, and much can happen along the way.

A moment's reflection shows that the problem pertains equally to quantitative work. Yes, the reader was not there to evaluate for himself what may have actually transpired during a qualitative field research encounter. But nor was the reader there when the quantitative researcher decided which items not to report from a long survey, "cleaned" the data on the chosen items, ran some analyses and not others (likely selecting those that made the results stand out the best), and wrote the output from the computer down into a research article, supposedly without lying about what the computer actually indicated. The specter of unjustified manipulation applies in quantitative work too. Plus, a new survey run by an investigator generally differs substantially in the topics of the questions, the wording of the questions, and the order of the questions—as well as the population to whom the questions are posed. Why? Because the intent of a new survey is to get at something previous surveys did not. So quantitative data collection instruments also vary significantly from investigator to investigator, study to study.

Because of these issues, scholars often dispute one another's results and insist on peer review of all work published in scholarly journals and books, whether the work is qualitative or quantitative. The difference between qualitative and quantitative research on the question of whether the work is fiction or not is mostly a difference in the degree to which these approaches call upon the cultural resources of positivist philosophy to handle the doubts and suspicions raised by the We voice.

Positivistic research characteristically responds with strategies of ***incontestability***—making the work indisputable through narratives of universalism, inaccessibility, and authority. It smooths over the rough and fuzzy edges of a categorical claim by applying it everywhere, minus a few local issues of poor measurement and unusual circumstance—puzzles that the reader is expected to tolerate as a matter of the ongoing state of our science. It obscures the feeling of the researcher as a person, with all her foibles, immanent in the work, by never mentioning her except in a by-line. It uses the narrative devices of the physicist and the chemist and the biologist, writing with passive constructions that eliminate the grammatical presence of an agent behind the doing of the research, and using specialized language and techniques that few readers will be able to fully understand. In these ways, positivism gains a transcendent, almost god-like narrative height that gives a sense of rightness—a view of everywhere that comes from nowhere, of all time that comes from no time, of all contexts that has no context of its own.

Multilogical work, however, deals with the doubts and concerns of the We not by claiming that no one can disagree with the work, but rather by claiming that anyone can disagree with the work. Multilogical research answers the question of how the work is scientific by making it disputable from a wide range of perspectives. It is open to others and welcomes reasoned debate.

Multilogical science is what we might call, with a bit of a smile, *disagreeable science*—that is, science that invites the reader to register any disagreement, science that enables disagreement through the way the researcher constructs the narrative, and science that shows the result of working through much disagreement in coming up with its interpretations. Multilogical science isn't afraid of challenge. In fact, the multilogical researcher considers himself lucky if his work merits enough attention for someone to want to dispute it. Because the multilogical researcher knows that there is so much that goes into producing research—multiplicity, singularity, positionality, narrativity—she welcomes another reasoned point of view, someone who might make those choices differently and is willing to explain why. For through such welcome, we move our understanding further along by bringing other logics into the conversation.

In order to get to that point, though, you have to open up a dialogue on your work and provide ways and entrance points for others to disagree with it. You need to give your work ***external contestability***—making your work understandable to a broad readership by providing enough detail and context to enable others to potentially interpret your results differently. And you need to give your work ***internal contestability***—deepen its contextuality by showing the range of difference within the categories of your work and the many perspectives on them among your research participants, rather than presenting a social world with no grey areas and no tensions. Internal contestability supports external contestability by giving the reader a more realistic account of the inevitable messiness of results.

Qualitative researchers have long stressed several techniques for giving their work internal contestability: *triangulation*, ***heteroglossia***, and ***disconfirmation***. Triangulation means that you make sure you provide different events, different research participants, different kinds of data, and different questions that let you see your results from multiple angles. Field research is especially valuable for its ability to triangulate between varying voices, scenes, and forms of evidence, from interviews to observation to documents. Heteroglossia means having more than one voice in the work. Make sure that, in addition to your own voice, you let the voices of different participants come through. Have different kinds of participant speaking. Have them have an internal conversation. Show internal diversity and difference. Disconfirmation means that you should not be afraid to present situations in which you were initially wrong, showing your own shifting perspectives on the work and the logic by which you interpreted your results—the contest internal to your own scientific reasoning. By showing mistakes and times you were wrong, you also make it clear that you are human and that the information you present is well thought out.

In addition to presenting internal contestability, you encourage external contestability by making your work accessible. If readers can't understand you, they won't be able to move science along through good discussion. We scholars want to be smart, which is not an unworthy motive. But we often try to sound smart by being un-understandable, according to the cultural theory that smart ideas must be the ones that are hard to understand. The multilogical scholar, however, wants his smartness to be tested and improved through discussion with others who understand his work. That includes one's research participants. If your participants can't understand anything about the work, it seems unlikely that they'll be able to contest your interpretation of their lives and lend science the lay scholarship of their everyday living.

So how can you challenge your interpretations and make them scientific? *By making them disputable from a wide range of perspectives, including both internal contestability and external contestability.* For the multilogical approach does not seek final truths. Rather, it offers a vision of the world which is unfinished, what Mikhail Bakhtin called "unfinalizable," open to more voices that give more sides to the truth, making it larger, more interesting, and more multilogical.[1]

Extendability

OK, so now your work is more than "just your interpretation," because of the reasoned confluence of voices within it and outside of it. But do your results matter for any situation other than the one you studied? Field research is inevitably based on a limited number of places and social interactions. It is what we might call "low-*n*" research, as opposed to the "high-*n*" of quantitative work. It is low in another sense too: It is close to the ground, from where one can get an excellent view of what is going on, as opposed to viewed from on high, when details get obscured. But many will wonder what its relevance is for another situation someplace else. So how will you answer the question raised by extendability—the question of the significance of your low-*n* work for elsewhere?

The question of extendability is usually referred to in research as the question of whether one's results are "generalizable." For the multilogical field researcher, however, the term generalizable is not entirely apt. At least, it has a history of usage which is not entirely apt, for the culture of research tends to immediately associate it with positivist claims of universality and permanence, of spatial and temporal transcendence, of replication. This kind of confident perspective is hard to maintain when our forms of evidence bring us close to the lived reality of social life, with its chaos, confusion, surprise, and infinite points of difference. Nothing ever exactly repeats itself, and no one is exactly the same as anyone else, as we discussed earlier in this book. Indeed, no one person ever exactly repeats herself or is exactly the same between one day to the next. Life is always varying and unfolding. Qualitative field methods bring out the resistance of the social to the categories in which we might like to cage it.

Well, that's not very helpful, you might want to say in response. Why should we do research if everything is different?

Precisely because it is, or we would understand it all already. Looking at science through the lens of replication misframes the value of good research. Just because everyone and every place and every time is at least just a little different does not mean that what happens to people in one place and time is irrelevant to what happens to them elsewhere and else when. There are indeed points of connection, common social flows, and related histories. Although water never courses down a stream in exactly the same array of splashes, waves, and undercurrents, we may still recognize it as a stream and trace its movement from place to place and time to time. Now imagine tracing three, four, five, or even a hundred streams pouring through one and the same location, colliding with each other, emptying into each other, blending into new streams with each other, and you'll have some sort of picture of the welter of the social. In a multilogical approach to research, we seek to identify the streams running awash across our research localities, perhaps issuing into a few new ones that other researchers had not noticed before. We see their directionality, so we are confident that there is intercontextuality in the context, that what we see in our research does have extensions beyond it, both upstream and downstream. But we do not presume that the flows will interact in exactly the same way elsewhere or will not intersect with some flows that were not present in our own research. Indeed, we doubt that they will interact in exactly the same way elsewhere.

We (that is; Mike and Jason, the authors) don't argue that we should necessarily throw out the word "generalize." It is too deeply sunk into the groundwater of research culture for that. But we do think that we at least need to shift from a replication metaphor for the word "generalize" to something like our metaphor of streams extending through the social, emphasizing that we do not have to sacrifice our appreciation of difference to order to gain an understanding of connection and consequence. This is what we mean by "extendability."[2]

Maybe it would help clarify our point to go back to a term from earlier: the notion of the "**presentedness**" of our research population versus its **representativeness.** Think of tracing those streams as identifying what social currents are present in the cases we study, and which are not, or only weakly, present. To do so, we need as full an understanding of the contextuality and intercontextuality of our study, in all its uniqueness and difference, as is reasonable to expect an author or a group of authors to achieve, given the constraining currents of their own lives. To put it another way, *we generalize by being as specific as possible*. When we know what is going on and what is not going on in a specific social situation, we can then compare it with what we know to be going on and not going on in another, extending contexts into other settings—into what we might call *intercontexts*, contexts that extend from one setting to another, acknowledging that they will likely manifest differently in different settings due to the interactions they encounter in each locale.

As specific as possible: No one will ever do a complete job. There is too much multiplicity in social life for that, as we discussed earlier. Besides, the authors had their own reasons for conducting their study, and their own positional advantages and disadvantages, without which they likely never would have achieved sufficient focus to call the work "done" and ready to turn into a contestable narrative. In this sense, it is the specifics that allow us to see both what is there and not there in the study, making it possible for us to see its connections and disconnections with other social locations.

And making it possible for others to do so as well.

You also don't want to do a complete job—if by complete you mean taking into account all possible factors such that you could have made a perfect prediction of what you encountered, one that others could use to make a perfect prediction in other contexts. Social life isn't like that. People are not machines. We're not replicated on an assembly line. So when you generalize by extending, make space for appreciating that people often surprise each other—and researchers. It's not necessarily a fault of theory that you encountered the unexpected. Indeed, certain contexts and intercontexts promote, perhaps even welcome, unexpected outcomes. Maybe you're studying jazz improvization. Maybe you're looking at a situation with a lot of conflict and struggle. Maybe there are—in fact, almost certainly there are—a multiplicity of logics at play, and they don't all fit neatly together for those in the situation. Thinking through the extent to which your research setting promotes the unexpected allows you to explain why some of your results are, well, maybe a bit strange. Call it *strange explanation*, a key aspect of multilogical research.[3]

So how will you make the case that your low-*n* research is broadly significant and worth paying attention to? *By contextualizing and intercontextualizing your research and showing what is presented in it and what is not.*

Generalization as extendability versus generalization as replication is more likely to inspire others, and make social life seem less like an imprisoning cage. It inspires the audience to take up the lines of inquiry that your work indicates, for it does not claim that all the work is done. It inspires people to see these lines of flow and to connect them to their own varied situations. It inspires people to extend the streams of sociality to themselves—and to have hope that, if need be, they might be able to change the flow of the streams and their consequences for others.

RECIPES FOR THE *WE* VOICE

1. TRIANGULATION

Triangulation is the process of verifying information by discovering it through another source. If you find it in another instance or through another method, then the information seems more likely to be correct. Furthermore, you can get a more detailed picture—like how a square becomes a cube when you add another dimension.

In your project, what kinds of triangulation will you use? We tend to use all of them.

Question triangulation: Survey researchers know that you often have to ask someone a question multiple times in different ways to get to "the truth." In an interview, for instance, Jason might ask someone a question at the beginning of the interview in one way, and then in a different way near the end. If their answers differ, he can ask them about the inconsistency, which is often due to the sensitive nature of the question or rapport.

Participant triangulation: Play participants off of each other. Does what one person said conflict with what someone else said? Ask them about it. Why would they have different points of view? Of course, they both can be right, but you will hear more in their responses that reveal answers to your research questions.

Method triangulation: Typically, this is the kind of triangulation that people think of when they hear the term. What different sources of data will you use? Asking questions in interviews about observations can produce rich answers.

2. Heteroglossia

The strength of qualitative fieldwork lies in many voices in dialogue, triangulating on what's present. Through heteroglossia, you build contestability by showing that different kinds of participants, different voices from different groups, are present.

Heteroglossia is not about overwhelming the audience, beating them into submission by giving them quote after quote after quote. Rather, it is about demonstrating the diversity present within your sample. The disagreements you heard between participants or spaces. It lets you present voices other than your own. These tools convince your audience that you are a reputable scholar, that you sought out and considered different perspectives.

3. Disconfirmation

You aren't always going to get it right. That's ok! Sometimes, you can learn more from your errors than from the times when you did everything by the book. Invisible narrativity though often tricks authors into not discussing their mistakes, or times in which they changed their mind. We want to know that your participants taught you something! If your participants hadn't changed your view at all, then we wouldn't be convinced that you had truly listened. Or, your topic was so bland or known that it didn't need to have a project devoted to it. Your topic isn't like that. You are going to change your mind. You are going to get things wrong. Tell us about them.

4. Accessibility

Different audiences require different strategies to make your work accessible. Sometimes, a single document, article, or book will not be accessible to all of your potential audiences equally. Consider the list of narratives that you generated in the exercise on audiences. Choose two. What venues would you have to publish or present in to access those two audiences? What approach to writing would be most effective for each audience? External contestability, and the ability of others to extend your work to new contexts, depends on different groups being able to understand and critique your work.

5. Extending

Even more than the other recipes in this section, extendability is something that you must return to constantly throughout the life course of a project. As we discussed, generalizability is only one way of understanding the flow from one project to the next. Extendability brings us full circle, connecting your project through intercontextuality back to the many streams that compose it. The findings of a project are important to all three voices of qualitative research. In this exercise, we'll consider how each group might use the findings.

For each of the three voices of multilogical research below, consider the next steps each group will take to extend or take up the lines of inquiry your project indicates. Both so-called pure knowledge and practical applications are important.

They: How will your project have a meaningful impact on the lives of the community you are studying? Given your project's findings or hypothesized findings, what might the community itself want the next research project that studies this community to involve?

You: A project is not only practically useful to your participants, but it will also influence your own life. What will you do differently in your own life given the findings or hypothesized findings of your study? How is this project only one part of the stream of your research agenda?

We: The audiences of your project are going to ask "So what?" early and often. What social issue or policy problem runs through your project? What is the disciplinary debate that your project intercedes in? What new lines of inquiry are available to others because of your work?

6. Unfinalizability

Mikhail Bakhtin offers in his work a vision of the world that is unfinished, willing to change, open to newness. Nothing is ever final nor would we want it to be. The sun keeps shining. The world keeps spinning. Your work, if you should be so lucky, will be discussed by others, critiqued, and, perhaps, one day discarded. We don't want to be the last word.

One way to encourage unfinalizability, and consequently build contestability and encourage extendibility, is to show areas where your project wasn't the best. These weaknesses are common in journal articles and reports. However, they are usually presented defensively as areas that don't matter to your argument or groups that others should study to test your ideas. Instead, present areas to which others could contribute their perspective. What improvements could be made on your design? This won't be your, or anyone's, last word on the topic.

Ways of Gathering

During the interview, Joyce and Troy presented two very different perceptions about
life, especially the time pressures and home life that farm life engendered. At one point
Mike, just after Joyce had come downstairs yet again from tending to the children,
attempted to change the subject to include her in the interview more. "What would yo
say your ideal farm would be?" asked Mike. They both hesitated, leading Mike to blur
perhaps overly personal question, "I mean, I guess you're in farming because you want
be, right?" Exactly the kind of leading question that awkward power situations can lea
Troy immediately said, "uh huh." But Joyce answered, "Or if you marry a person who i
In the awkwardness that followed– was Joyce rejecting farm life that came with Troy
the two of them alternatively dis d from the interview, letting the other one spe
while they ignored the other a h the baby. The dynamics between Joyce
Troy revealed as much as th y had said. If Mike had interviewed th
separately, perhaps Joyce bout about Troy's sche
and the strain in their fa this situation a
agonistic element for ard conversa
an interac e in this te
- like sence fr

5
LISTENING
Interview Methods

Jason's first interview went terribly.

"I'm sure there is a place around here somewhere." Jason had assured Amy, a bright young student that he was interviewing about her campus organization. Naively, Jason thought that he could just show up. They would just hop into an empty quiet room in the Student Union and she would pour out all of the information he was hoping to get about student political involvement.

But listening is hard.

It took 10 minutes, with Amy at least remaining chipper, following behind Jason as he tried every set of locked doors in the dizzying twisting halls of the Union. Eventually, he found a table in the dining area, about five feet away from sporadically yelling undergrads. Needless to say, transcribing that interview later was difficult. To make matters worse, his interview guide was sporadically organized. Unsure at times what he wanted to focus on, Amy spent large portions of the interview telling stories that Jason thought were off-topic and he never ended up using.

Mike once had the opposite experience. The most difficult-to-reach people in fieldwork are generally those most unlike yourself. If you're middle class, the very poor and the very rich will likely be the hardest for you. So Mike was thrilled to get an interview with a genuine aristocrat who was living in the village in England where he conducted his dissertation research. And the interview went great. Much to Mike's amazement, Sir Maynard, a baronet, was very forthcoming about the troubles of life, as he saw them. He said many very quotable things—indeed, some quite shocking things. But Mike was not able to use one of them: He had left the recorder on pause for the entire interview.[1]

These days, with a lot more experience, the skills for interviewing have become second nature for Jason and Mike. But interviewing isn't just a matter of logistics. Unfortunately, one can't just show up and expect participants to tell rich stories and provide in-depth information. For every minute spent in the interview, the researcher spends many more preparing beforehand and analyzing afterwards.

In this chapter, we broadly discuss the necessary preparation and skills needed for quality qualitative interviewing before, during, and after the interview. Like all the methods described in this middle section of the book, listening is a method that can stand on its own or mix with other qualitative (or quantitative!) methods as necessary to answer the research questions proposed. Listening is also a skill that improves the methods we discuss later: ethnographic and participatory methods. Listening—truly listening—is the foundation of fieldwork methods because it allows the They voice to come through in a project. While methods like ethnography and participation might more easily allow the They voice of a project to come through in respondents' own words, listening is the most traditional and widespread technique.

The recipes at the end of the chapter provide exercises for building interviewing skills and guides to setting up key portions of an interview project.

Before the Interview

As we mentioned in chapter 2, most people think of the process of locating participants for a study, especially an interview project, backwards. Before one worries about recruitment strategies, however, one must first develop a coherent population narrative—your explanation for why it makes sense for you to focus your research on the population or populations you choose and not on others. But a population is usually bigger than you can hope to cover completely and is always filled with huge diversity (if, in fact, you really are listening). If your work focuses on an issue of broad significance, you can't talk to everyone who has something to say about it. You simply can't. So how are you going to decide whom to talk to (and whom not to) and still ensure that your "low-*n*" sample is comprehensive?

Theoretical sampling

The key technique of the multilogical fieldworker is, to borrow a tip from grounded theory methods, ***theoretical sampling***. Theoretical sampling means that we choose our participants based on theoretical reasons. Rather than attempting to achieve a representative sample from the population, as one might in statistical research, theoretical sampling seeks what chapters 2 and 4 called "presentedness." You want to be able to gauge the multiplicity and singularity present in your case, in its full diversity and uniqueness, whether that case is a group, a problem, or a neighborhood. You want to be able to say what is going on in your case, and what is not. Theoretical sampling is the process of continually refining whom we are going to talk to based on our emerging understanding of a case's dynamics so that we can best determine what is present—what its presentedness is.

Theoretically sampling a population doesn't mean that we enter a population wildly, just picking whomever strikes our fancy. Because You as the researcher already have ideas from scholarly training, literature, and personal experience, it is possible to come up with a sampling frame that corresponds to the population narrative that you have already developed. When considering the multiplicity and singularity of your case, you developed the population narrative that introduced a contrast or comparison or identified key demographic characteristics that would inform you about your case. A sampling frame turns that population narrative into a table with an approximate number of people that will fit into each cell (as in the recipe on p. 89). This table guides your recruitment efforts, ensures that you talk to all the different points of view.

A theoretical sampling frame is never absolute and finished, though. A project is going to change as you acquire more information. The They voice of your research is going to point you towards new avenues, new contrasts, new comparisons. As we like to say to students, if you haven't learnt something new that changes your project, then you haven't been listening! While researchers often present their work narratively as though they knew their final sampling frame from the beginning, that's a trick of positivistic writing styles. You aren't doing anything wrong if you change things in the middle of your project. A good qualitative interviewing project is going to listen to the participants and follow their lead to new kinds of people to interview.

Central to theoretical sampling is constantly challenging your emerging interpretations. The most important practice in making your work contestable, as we termed it in chapter 4, is to contest yourself. If you are starting to see a pattern, ask yourself how might someone with a different social location experience things differently. Then go try to connect with someone like that and ask them. And don't be disappointed if they tell you something different from what others told you, thus apparently trashing your emerging theory. In multilogical fieldwork, we expect that people who are differently located will see things through different logics, logics that emerge from their different experiences. Instead of discovering your error, you learn that there are more facets to the situation, allowing you to cut the jewel of your theory into a more glittering brilliance.[2]

Theoretical sampling can be a never-ending rabbit hole, however. When are you finished? There are always new paths to take and there are always new people. It's called "sampling," after all. If you talked to everyone in the population, then it would be a census—and it wouldn't be very thorough. Besides, talking to everyone is an impossibility. As multiplicity teaches us, there are an infinite number of contexts that run through our case. To follow all these leads is impossible and takes you off track. Although there are an infinite number of contexts, not all will be equally significant for your research problem.

But here's a bit of good news: Infinity is not the same as everything. You can have infinite variety within the dynamics that are present in a case and still be able to determine that many more dynamics simply aren't present at all, or hardly at all. The World Cup may catch the interest of billions of people from around the world, with hugely varied reactions to the outcomes of a game. But they aren't playing baseball out there.

And here's some more good news: Theoretical sampling leads eventually to a point of diminishing returns. This point is called ***theoretical saturation***. People often define saturation as the point when you aren't learning anything new. That's an over-statement. There will always be new things to learn, especially if we are asking the right questions. Perfect saturation is impossible. However, eventually, more interviews and listening to more people is going to be largely repetitive. There will be no new major theoretical developments. You'll have discovered the important dynamics that are present in your case.

It may surprise you to know that you can reach saturation on some topics fairly quickly. When Greg Guest, Arwen Bunce, and Laura Johnson finished collecting 60 interviews in West Africa for a large qualitative interview project, they went back and analyzed their notes and memos. When did the majority of theoretical developments stop? At what point did all the themes they would eventually use appear in their notes?

After 12 interviews.

For the basics, they found as few as six interviews gave them the necessary information.[3]

Few scholars though, especially of a positivistic bent, are going to trust your work if you only collect six interviews. Some academic audiences will be fine with 15. Others, 25. Some journals, such as the *Archives of Sexual Behavior*, have published minimums under which they won't accept a piece. Others have informal requirements. These requirements are not merely arbitrary. Additional interviews will give your work a sufficient number of voices—heteroglossia, again!—to make it contestable. You must convince your audience that your work represents a novel, relevant, and accurate answer.

Furthermore, it can take some time before you realize that you have reached saturation. It takes a few interviews where you hear much the same thing—where you don't have much luck coming up with questions or with people telling you something significantly different or unexpected—before you can be sure that you should stop collecting interviews. That's one reason that interview analysis and coding, discussed later in the chapter, should happen before, between, and after interviews. To know that you are finished with interviewing, you must constantly test your ideas.

However, don't simply collect more interviews for the sake of collecting them. Fetishizing a large number of participants in your method section is burdensome on the population you are studying. For most research questions, we recommend planning for between 20 and 30 one to two-hour in-depth interviews, yielding 30 to 40 hours of material. If your question is large, complex, and wide-ranging, then you might need more. If you are asking specific questions of a small population, you might need less. Keep track of the theoretical development of your project. That, more than any strict number of participants, will enhance the quality and credibility of your project.

Recruitment

Once you've made a sampling frame, it is time to start thinking of recruitment. Different recruitment techniques often have the term sampling in them, but don't confuse them with the overall strategy that you will be using.

The most common type of recruitment strategy for qualitative fieldwork projects is "snowball sampling," which we prefer to call ***relational recruiting***. It's more accurate. Relational recruiting leverages the social networks of your participants to reach people who you would not otherwise be in contact with. Consistent with theoretical sampling, ask participants at the end of the interview for specific kinds of people you are looking for, as per your sampling frame.

If they have trouble thinking of people, try these three questions: Who would disagree with your answers to today's questions? Whom do you know who is very different from you? Who might be interested, but you are not very close to? These questions will allow you to seek disconfirmation, people who will challenge your preconceived notions or emerging explanation. At least, these questions will get you further out of the social network of that participant, widening your reach.

Some might argue that relational recruiting will generate a biased and inaccurate representation of the population or community's views. Again, qualitative multilogical projects focus on presentedness, continually answering new questions until saturation is reached and you've made your work contestable. However, it can be important to know that you'll likely reach the different kinds of people in a community, even if the sample is not strictly random or representative.

Respondent-driven sampling (RDS) is a specific, non-theoretically driven, sampling method that attempts to estimate representative populations based on the kinds of network-based recruitment that we have described. Similar to relational recruitment, an RDS project begins with a number of "seeds" and these seeds then recruit three members of their social network, who then do the same. Population researchers have used this method successfully to construct representative samples of small, hidden, or stigmatized populations. For instance, Carey Johnson and her colleagues at the Fenway Institute found, using RDS after three waves of recruitment, that their sample matched the key racial demographics of their population, HIV+ men, despite the usual difficulty of finding these men.[4] For our purposes, it is not important to mimic the techniques of RDS in terms of evaluating our sample as statistically representative of the population that we are sampling from. But the success of social network-driven recruitment should alleviate our concerns that we are going to miss key kinds of participants with relational recruiting that might matter to us theoretically.

Those "seed" participants, though, can be hard to find. All methods are going to involve some sort of gateway: a person, group, institution, or even area affiliated with the people you are targeting with your sampling frame. A few examples will probably be the most illustrative. Ethnographers, those using methods we discuss in the next chapter, *Looking*, probably have it easiest in this regard. Their method already involves immersing themselves in the groups and places that are relevant to their study. Mike was already living in "Childerley," the pseudonymous village in his book on the relationship between ideas of nature and ideas of class.[5] So he easily met people he might interview in the same spaces where he was observing British village life. The pubs, for example, provided a place where he could meet people who regularly hung out there. Mitchell Duneier, in *Sidewalk*, was already observing the daily lives of street vendors in New York City. He easily encountered potential interview participants during that activity, especially once he met his gatekeeper, Hakim, a street vendor he befriended (and whom we talk about in more detail in the last chapter).[6] In Japonica Brown-Saracino's *The Neighborhood that Never Changes*, she meets interviewees through attending meetings of neighborhood groups and business alliances in Chicago, Provincetown, and Dresden.[7]

Studies based only on methods of Listening and not Looking are going to have a harder time. The same principles apply, though. Access to initial seed interviews comes from recruiting people through the places where they are likely to be. If one is interested in women's role in family formation within African-American church communities, then putting up fliers all around a city is not likely to draw as many potential initial interviews as directed recruitment at African-American churches. Getting the approval of key parties within those churches, such as the pastor or deacons, is likely to bring you even more success, not to mention being more ethical.

This is likely why so many interview projects work with specific organizations that already serve the populations they are interested in. Interested in the recently incarcerated? Reintegration programs are your likely bet. Jason's work on coming out began with attending a meeting of a queer political organization at a local college.

However, examine your positionality. Some spaces and groups are going to be easier than others to gain access to. Most notably, since many researchers are affiliated with academic institutions, this can lead us to overly recruit college students for our projects. After all, they are right there sitting in our classes, whether next to us as students or under our supervision as professors. Relational recruiting is even more important in these circumstances. Seeking disconfirmation through theoretical sampling should inevitably lead one out of and beyond the social networks we have easy access to and into those that our positionality might make it hard to access.

But once you've located and recruited your participants, the work has just begun. Now, you actually have to interview them.

During the Interview

Interviews are tiring.

Active listening, the kind that you must do during interviews to respect your participants and to collect high quality data, is mentally draining. It requires your full attention at all times. Conversations don't usually have large gaps and most people are uncomfortable with the one-sidedness of the typical interview. They require constant affirmation that you are listening through nods and proper questions—verbal, and physical cues. (Although not so much that you look like a bobble head!)

But there are also many tasks that you simultaneously have to do. You'll be taking notes while also selecting the next question off of your interview guide, fashioning the proper probes, comparing this interviewee's responses to previous interviews, and navigating power relations.

As the interview unfolds, you'll also have to navigate the trickiness of asking personal questions and hearing confessional tales. Recall the social position of the stranger, which we discussed in chapter 3.[8] When a stranger comes into a situation, they may be distrusted and stigmatized. But they are also someone who is outside of that group's internal conflict, drama, and strife. Because they are on the outside, and perhaps not going to stay for long, the stranger can take on a confessor role for people. Imagine a traveler sitting at a bar. This person isn't involved in anything touching you. They are also unlikely to be able to have any influence over your situation. Yet, many people when talking to this person might confide personal details or tell stories that they would not normally divulge. The social distance means that you can talk to them about things you wouldn't confess to anyone else. For Catholics before Vatican II, the physical barrier in the confessional attempted to create a kind of stranger out of a priest who would otherwise be known to them.

Interviewers and researchers are often strangers to the contexts they study. Even someone heavily involved in a community, whether because of their positionality or because they are using participatory methods (see chapter 7), still must navigate and maintain as best they can this delicate stranger role. If you are interested in listening to someone's life and social world—as most fieldworkers are—then you are relying on them telling you about it. You are asking them questions that they might not discuss with anyone else.

And they will gladly tell you about it. For instance, people often assume that sexuality researchers, like Jason, have a difficult time getting people to tell them about their sex lives. After all, although people talk about sex all the time in the mass media, many people do not tell others about the intimate details of their desires and sexual activities. However, as a stranger, researchers are told such information precisely because people don't often get the opportunity to talk about such issues with others. As one of our close friends, a therapist, told us: "Half of what I do is listen as though a close friend, but outside of the situation."

However, you have to be able to ride the line between being a stranger and being a therapist to interviewees. Even trained therapists, like Gloria Gonzalez-Lopez, do not engage in therapy during research interviews. While women and men told her many traumatic stories during interviews for her book *Erotic Journeys*, she refrained from counseling them in the manner of a therapist.[9] Being empathic and actively listening to someone is different from the engaged work of a therapist. González-López paused the tape recorder often, providing the name of another therapist, to work through the traumatic events they experienced. Although you'll occupy the social position of the stranger, it is disrespectful to them to allow the interview space, which you are going to use as data, to become a therapy session—an important issue of the ethics of interviewing.

Interview Guides and Probing

Two key interviewing techniques—carefully constructed ***interview guides*** and ***probing***—can help navigate the space of the stranger and prevent confessional tales from becoming counseling sessions. Both of these shift people away from only relating personal anecdotes and towards the reflection that will be most useful to you as data.

An interview guide is, at its simplest, a list of topics that you are going to discuss during your interview. An interview guide keeps you on track during the interview. In an hour-long discussion, without an interview guide you'll either let the participant ramble on or sit in awkward silence fumbling for a question. The type of interview guide you use will depend on the type of interview you want to conduct: *structured*, *co-constructed*, or *unstructured*. Recipes for each type can be found at the end of the chapter.

A **structured interview** attempts to keep each interview as similar as possible to allow direct comparison of participants' answers. Extremely structured interviews are not even really a matter of Listening; they are more like oral surveys than conversations. Most structured interviews use an ordered set of questions that guide each participant through the same questions, using the same or similar probes for each topic. The interview starts with several questions designed to take the interview progressively deeper and make it more personal. The interview ends similarly lightly. A structured interview is most appropriate for topics where you need descriptive information or where the topic is so sensitive that you must carefully guide an interviewee through the topic in case they shut down.

A **co-constructed interview**—also often called a "semi-structured" interview—is more participant-driven.[10] The interview guide still lists questions, but more of the interview time is spent following the topics that participants bring up. The ordering and exact wording of the questions differ between interviews, putting more emphasis on thematic comparisons than direct comparison of answers. These interview guides list general questions that you can use to pick up the conversation when it is lagging. We find co-constructed interviews to be best for most topics, since they invite participants to share in the process of the interview, often alerting the researcher to important matters she might not have thought to ask about but without her abandoning control over the course of the interview completely.

An **unstructured interview** is the most participant-driven. But even these interviews have room for an interview guide. An unstructured interview proposes a topic and then lets the participant guide the subjects that will be discussed. An interview guide for this kind of interview might list different topics that one wants to hit on during the interview. These kinds of interviews are great when very little is known about the topic or where the entire point of the interviews is to gauge the topics of importance for that population. We suggest them for investigators at the very beginning of their work.

In other words, not all the interviews for a project need use the same style of interview. And they likely won't use the same interview guide. You'll edit your interview guide for different kinds of participants and reshape it according to the theoretical development of the project. Depending on the topic and your previous knowledge, the first few interviews might be unstructured, to gauge the kinds of responses to the topic and map the contours of your research question. Or you might have very specific descriptive questions that must be answered before you can begin developing the theoretical argument. Then a structured interview might be most useful. The middle of the project will likely use co-constructed interview guides, since you know the general topics but need participants to lead you through and flesh them out and alert you to important matters that you may still have overlooked. At the end of a project, when you know the most, you might actually use structured interviews again, asking participants specific questions that fill out the information you still need rather than only telling you stories you've heard before.

In every type of interview, probing is the most important skill. Probes are the follow-up questions that shape your interviewee's responses into useful data. These follow-up questions ask participants to elaborate on something that they said. Probes must be delivered at the appropriate moment and correspond to the right level. As with most skills, practice is the best method for improving. The best moments for probes are when the conversation seems to be lagging, when respondents are rambling or unclear, or when it seems they are referring to unspoken knowledge. In each of these instances, a probe focuses the conversation to ensure that every moment is building your knowledge rather than "just talking."

Leveling is a probing technique whereby you shift an interviewee towards another mode of thinking to access additional information. As shown in Table 5.1,[11] one can think of an interview as having three levels of discussion and four time periods. Moving an interviewee between these gets her to assess a situation from different vantage points, potentially getting new information. Most novice interviewers tend to only ask feeling questions—"How did that make you feel?" or "What is your opinion about X?"—which can produce very shallow answers. If someone is only talking at the level of their opinions, moving them up or down a level can cause them to give a more in-depth answer. For instance, "Tell me a story of a time that you felt that way" would put respondents in a narrative space that might reveal additional dimensions to you that they might not consciously articulate. Similarly, if they are providing an anecdote, a well-timed theorizing hypothetical like "What would other people do in that situation?" could reveal spots where they think that their behavior was unique, context dependent, or otherwise different from what they perceive is the standard response. Leveling allows you to sort through the multiplicity and singularity within their responses. Rather than analysis being something that only you conduct, leveling brings your participants in to help.

Effective probes also ask participants to compare their experience with that of previous interviewees: "Another person I interviewed didn't say anything when they heard a racist comment; what would you do in that situation?" Although leading on the surface, this question gives

Table 5.1 Interview Matrix

		Levels of Abstraction			
		Past	Present	Future	Hypothetical
Question Focus	Narratives/Experiences				
	Opinions/Feelings/Facts				
	Theorizing				

participants permission to answer in two different ways. Asking questions in this way gives them space to disagree—Of course, I would say something!—or agree, especially if it is embarrassing or socially unacceptable to have done so—um, yea, I've never done that either. Using these kinds of probes is especially effective as a project nears saturation. Asking, "Some participants experience X; what has been your experience?" can determine whether there are additional possibilities out there.

Sometimes, the proper probe is to disagree with a participant. This is called an *agonistic question*. Most novice interviewers, concerned with keeping a rapport with their participants, agree with nearly everything they say. At most, they might speak neutrally. Sometimes, though, asking a challenging question or even disagreeing or asking a question that implies disagreement prompts a participant to defend their statement, giving you more information than you would otherwise get. It can also build rapport, a sign of active listening that indicates you are taking what the interviewee says seriously. The trick is to ask the question in such a way that it does not indicate a challenge to the person's identity or status, only to the information the person has given. As you will know from your experiences in everyday life, this can be a difficult line to walk. So you should use **agonistic questioning** cautiously. You are a researcher, not a gotcha journalist or talk show host.

Power Relations in an Interview

You must also be wary of the power dynamics within the interview, whether you're using agonistic interviewing or not. No matter what your positionality, you're not going to share all identities with your participants. That can create power differentials, if only because you're a researcher with the power of leading the conversation and asking questions. Often, we only consider the situation where we have more power than participants. In that situation, it is important to allow space for the participant to guide the interview—as in unstructured interviews—or to disagree with you.

However, you must also be wary of the power difference when interviewing elites, called "interviewing up." It can be tempting to let elites run the show during an interview, for fear that they will cut off access or that we will ruin the rapport if we disagree with them. But those situations can actually be the most useful for agonistic interviewing. For example, Mike used agonistic methods extensively in his lost interview with Sir Maynard, who loved it. Probably due in part to his elite status, Sir Maynard did not feel threatened when Mike asked a challenging question. As long as it is respectful disagreement that does not threaten a person's status or identity, a challenging question can jolt interviewees out of giving you the "response set"— the answer that they believe that you want to hear. They may also delight in the repartee, as long as it comes with an air of fun or other non-threatening emotion.

Multi-participant interviews, including focus groups, have their own power relations. These too can be helpful, since the dynamics amongst the participants can often reveal as much as the words that they are saying. So much of Listening is getting out of the way during your interviews and actually listening. A perfect example comes from Mike's second ethnography, *Farming for Us All*, when he sat down to interview a young couple, Troy and Joyce, at their family farm. Sitting in their kitchen at 8 p.m., Joyce had to keep getting up from the interview to settle their four young children into their bedtime routine. During the interview, Joyce and Troy presented two very different perceptions about farm life, especially the time pressures on home life that farm life engendered. At one point, just after Joyce had come downstairs yet again from tending to the children, Mike attempted to change the subject to include her in the interview more. "What would you say your ideal farm would be?" asked Mike. They both hesitated, leading Mike to blurt out a perhaps overly personal question, "I mean, I guess you're in farming because you want to be, right?"

Troy immediately said, "Uh huh."

But Joyce answered, "Or if you marry a person who is?"

In the awkwardness that followed—was Joyce rejecting the farm life that came with Troy?—the two of them alternately disengaged from the interview, letting the other one speak while they ignored the other and played with the baby.

The dynamics between Joyce and Troy revealed as much as the words they used. If Mike had interviewed them separately, perhaps Joyce would have opened up about her concerns about Troy's schedule and the strain in their family. Or perhaps not. In this situation Troy seemed to serve as an agonistic element for her. As it was, Mike was able to see from this awkward conversation an interaction between gender and farm work, and the use of ideas of nature in this tension—like the way that Troy blamed his schedule on unpredictable weather (rain, for example) to frame his absence from home as outside of his control. In essence, although Mike was the interviewer, Joyce and Troy interviewed each other, responding to the other's implicit (and sometimes agonistic) questions.

Because of the potential for discomfort, it is not ethical to encourage such tensions in group interviews. But you should be prepared for them to arise, and be ready to use your social skills to navigate the group away from such moments as best you can. Fortunately, there are other ways to listen in on the crosstalk of daily life, and to allow interviewees to basically interview themselves. Especially in focus groups, we like to use the opportunity for probes to bring others into the conversation and invite interaction. (Don't address probes to the last person speaking, however. Address them to everyone, as a way to guide the discussion between participants.)

Informed Consent

The potential for situations like the one Mike encountered with Troy and Joyce is one of the reasons why Institutional Review Boards (IRBs) require researchers to ensure "informed consent" on the part of interviewees, in either oral or written form (and ideally both, where practical), except in very unusual circumstances. Awkward and possibly painful moments can equally well come up in one-on-one interviews too. It's just hard to know, even with a seemingly straightforward and non-controversial topic, what might touch a raw emotional nerve for someone, as we know from our own experience in everyday life.

Informed consent procedures are now pretty well standardized across the country. They always require the following elements of consent:

- that interviewees know they can stop an interview at any time;
- that interviewees know they can refuse the interview before it starts, even if they previously agreed to it;
- that interviewees know they can retract any interview content at any time, even long after the interview;

- that interviewees know if there is audio or video recording of the interview;
- that interviewees know the level and form of confidentially the researcher will provide;
- that interviewees know ahead of time how long the interview is expected to last;
- that interviewees know the potential risks and benefits of participating in the research.

These are sensible requirements. At the very least, they represent common courtesy and decency.

However, in many cases, you have to recognize that even if you provide confidentiality, there could be times when you are forced to provide government authorities with your field notes, interview transcripts, or other identifying details. This presents an ethical challenge that you should think out ahead of time! What are you going to do if someone reveals an illegal activity to you, such as a crime or drug use?

Be aware of your institution's mandatory reporting requirements. In many states in the USA, you are legally obliged to report child or elder abuse to authorities if you hear it in the course of research. Your participants have a right to know that you will be required to report them if they reveal such information to you.

However, what about other crimes? You need to decide upfront, in communication with your mentors and IRB, and let your participants know your decisions ahead of time. In many cases, you might choose to tell them that you will protect their identity, perhaps by destroying material or not producing field notes that list that activity. None of this offers protection from a government subpoena.

The National Institute of Health (NIH) recognized that research on illegal activities needed protection so that participants feel free to disclose drug use or other illegal activities that would influence their health. For this reason, some researchers qualify for "certificates of confidentiality." According to the guidelines, however, the research must fall within the purview of one of the mission areas of the NIH or its institutes. Thus, while fantastic protection for those who qualify, certificates of confidentiality are not an automatic solution to the ethical quandary. If you are collecting sensitive material and qualify, you should get one. If not, take other precautions to protect your participants' information.

Time and Place

The time and location of an interview is another important factor to bear in mind, for many reasons—including ethics and protection. Of course, you will want to base your choice on practical reasons of convenience for everyone involved. But the multilogical researcher realizes that the setting of an interview is part of its context and will shape its content. So we recommend letting the interviewees pick a spot and time that is convenient to them—with some important caveats.

Since they are not researchers, participants might not think of some of the considerations that are important to you. Will the noise level be conducive to tape recording? A coffee shop might be convenient, but trying to figure out later what someone said over the music or whistling espresso machine could be difficult. That said, Jason still conducts many of his interviews at coffee shops. He attempts to get around noise level issues by selecting secluded corners.

Interviews that happen in public spaces, like coffee shops, are going to be quite different, though, from ones held in the privacy of someone's home or their office or the private room of a library. When Jason was interviewing young people about their coming out experiences, these different spaces elicited quite different stories, so Jason made sure to vary the location. Interview evidence is contextual evidence. For instance, one participant, Martin, would probably not have discussed his childhood incest experience and the difficulty navigating coming out to family members who knew about it if they had been in a bustling coffee shop near the college campus where he was enrolled instead of a private room.

Yet interviews in public spaces can get equally important information about more everyday experiences. In Jason's work, this kind of contextual evidence wound up influencing his theory construction more perhaps than the sensitive personal stories. In short, varying the location can be beneficial. Just like you vary the other variables and questions for your project, consider theoretically what kind of information you need from a particular participant and suggest spaces to fit.

But you should also keep in mind your own safety. Interviewing can be a very intimate encounter. Interviewees sometimes get the wrong message. And sometimes they try to take advantage of the situation. Given sexism and sexual violence, women researchers should take special care when interviewing men. Alas, we know several women colleagues who have received unwelcome advances from male interviewees, including groping. Male researchers can receive unwelcome advances too, from both women and men, just as female researchers can also receive unwelcome advances from women. These are all deeply disturbing events for researchers. You place trust in the interviewee, just as the interviewee places trust in you. It is awful to have your trust violated—even more, your own person.

IRB guidelines do not cover the risks to the researcher, however. You will need to be wary on your own. Obviously, the setting of the interview will have a big impact on your own level of risk. If you have any doubts at all, make sure the interview is in a public location, despite the hazards of extraneous noise and the effect that a public setting may have on the content of the interview. And remember, you can refuse an interview too.

Bringing the Interview to a Conclusion

As the interview ends, you'll want to pull interviewees back out of the confessional space that was developed during the interview. This is also the opportunity to check with respondents that you've been discussing the appropriate information. We propose three kinds of questions.

First, Jason almost always says, "I've been peppering you with questions for the last hour, is there anything that you wanted to ask me?" There are a few ways in which interviewees usually respond to a question like that. They might ask you a personal question about the topics that you discussed during the interview, like asking Jason whether he is gay. They might ask you what led you to do work on this topic, leading you to reveal any personal connections or passions about the project. They might also ask you to explain what you're "really" interested in, since due to "deception contamination" many people assume that researchers are asking questions only tangentially related to the topic they are truly interested in. In general, we advise against deception in multilogical work. Participants know a lot about their situation. That's why you are interviewing them. Putting the reasoning behind your work into non-academic language both honors participants and gives them a further chance to help you understand their context. So this kind of question provides an opportunity for you to tell them about the scope and aims of the project.

Next, we ask a question to gauge whether there were unasked issues: "Given what we talked about today, what else could we have discussed?" Interviewees might not have anything else to bring up. But sometimes they have a ton. We find that this part of the interview can often take up almost a fourth of the total time. Participants will often bring up additional areas that are new to you and require extensive probing. Especially in a co-structured interview, this can be the most valuable question you ask—where you really learn something new, something that hadn't occurred to you before would be significant.

Last, it is important to ask about other potential participants. Using the questions above in discussing saturation, we ask participants to refer us through their social networks to new people. Depending on the requirements of your IRB, you'll either ask them to pass on your information to these potential participants or you'll collect their information in order to make contact yourself. If possible, get their information right then because collecting and tracking down new recruits can be quite difficult after the fact. In some communities, you may notice that participants will suggest the names of people you've already interviewed. Remember that if you promised those people confidentiality, you shouldn't tell anyone, even other people you've interviewed, whether you interviewed them or not.

Then, turning off the tape recorder and putting away your notepad, the interview is finally over.

After the Interview

Except the interview isn't really over. After you've turned the tape recorder off, interviewees will sometimes act as though a weight has been lifted from the conversation. While walking you out or while you're packing up your things, they'll often mention that "one more thing" that just occurred to them. This is also important data! Sometimes the very best! As soon as you get away from the interview space, record these interactions in your notes—although you will need to think carefully about whether the interviewee has implicitly given you permission to use this information. If you are unsure, ask.

It is extremely important to write up your notes about the interview as soon after the interview as possible. If too much time passes, you'll find the little details slipping from your memory. What did that respondent emphasize with her voice and body when speaking? What seemed especially important to your burgeoning analysis? What were the key topics? If you have to put off writing the notes for more than a few hours—driving quite a distance home from rural farms, for instance—then stop the car, turn the recorder back on, and take audio notes instead.

Summaries, Notes, and Analytical Memos

There are key parts to your interview write-up: the ***interview summary***, ***interview notes***, and ***analytical memos***. The interview summary is an executive summary of the key topics discussed during the interview. A year or two or ten after the interview, these notes will be your only guide to what is in this particular transcript or tape. This summary can also serve as an index to the key points of analysis that you will want to come back to later.

The interview notes focus on all the intangibles and the information that will not be in the recording. In addition to writing up the notes on the right side of your notepad, make notes of any other embodiment you want to remember from the interview. Discuss where the interview took place. Jason usually begins his notes with the story of how he met this participant and other information he might know about them from ethnographic observation. Mike will sometimes make a little map of the room and who sat where. If you have an artistic bent, perhaps make a sketch or caricature of the interviewee. Your interview notes should also include any information about positionality and reflexivity that you see influencing the interview.

Analytical memos are notes about the initial analysis of the interview. Are there themes in this interview that were new? How does this interview fit within your sampling frame and theoretical sampling? To assess saturation, discuss the ways that this interview is similar to and/or different from other interviews, especially those of the same type. These analytical memos are the space to write up any ideas the interview might have evoked about how to answer your research question.

Nota bene: IRB guidelines usually require you to immediately apply pseudonyms or numbers to respondents as soon as you take notes on an interview or make a transcript, lest someone gain access to your write-up. Even inadvertently—like passing by your table in the coffee shop and seeing a bit of your write-up on your computer screen while you're at the counter ordering a second cup. This requirement can be very confusing to the researcher, as our brains are long trained to store our experiences with others away in the grey, using their name as the retrieval cue. Change the names, and your mental hard disk can't find the data. You might think you'll remember, but a few interviews into a project and it all starts getting confused.

So what to do? One practice we recommend is asking interviewees to come up with their own pseudonyms, if they would like to. They generally do a great job, and it saves you a lot of hassle in thinking up something appropriate. But more importantly, the pseudonym becomes part of the research encounter. You'll remember the relationship between pseudonym and real name much more easily. Also, most interviewees enjoy the little moment of fantasizing another identity for themselves.

But however you come up with your pseudonyms, you'll need to keep a master list, so you don't scramble your data. Not on your computer, however. IRB guidelines often will require that you keep it in a separate location from your data. And you had best keep a back-up in yet a third place.

Coding and Memoing

After you've collected your first interview, and after every subsequent interview, you can start analyzing the data and developing some answers to your research questions. Most interviewers do this through a process of ***coding*** and ***memoing***.

Coding generates codes—thematic tags that describe a portion of the data—while memoing involves writing down your thoughts, summarizing themes, and comparing data between and within interviews. Grounded theory researchers, and those in the same lineage, like situational analysis, have developed specialized coding techniques and several computer programs to help with what can be a very time-consuming process. These researchers typically go through a process of ***open coding*** followed by ***focused coding***. Open coding focuses on generating themes by focusing on minute portions of their talk. A grounded theorist might work clause by clause, line by line, paragraph by paragraph, pulling out as many ideas and phrases as they can, some in vivo straight from the transcript in the participant's own words. Taking cues from the symbolic interactionist tradition, they focus on the work being done at micro-level with speech to indicate wider issues that speak to their theory.

Grounded theorists then take these to the analytical memos we discussed above, where the hundreds of open codes are combined into themes and categories. They attempt to explain the problem and develop a theory by continually comparing different pieces of data and refining their codes and categories. These final codes are then reapplied to the interviews through focused coding, the process of tagging all interviews with a similar list of themes, properties, and analytical categories to allow further comparison between the data.

While each of these techniques has its place, we feel that for most kinds of fieldwork the full process is not worth the investment of time and resources. It requires transcripts of all interviews, which is enormously time-consuming if you do it yourself and money-consuming if you don't. And that's only what you need to get going. Coding interviews is also extremely time-intensive. It also encourages a focus on codes over context, a more reductionist logic. Moreover, the work done at the focused coding level is seldom all used for publication and dissemination. And because of their roots in open coding and symbolic interaction, the codes can often focus too much on the social psychological dynamics of the participant, which is not key to all questions.

But for some research questions, a full-on grounded theory style of coding is very helpful, even essential. This is particularly the case for large-scale, multiple investigator projects taking place on many sites, using a less contextual logic of scholarship. We recommend classics like *Constructing Grounded Theory* by Kathy Charmaz if you're interested in working with a strict process.

Multilogical qualitative work, however, usually relies more heavily on analytical memos, using coding as needed to push us forward and return us to our participants' words. Write analytical memos often—a few types are included in the recipes at the end of the chapter—and share them with others. As you near theoretical saturation and have a clearer idea of the answers to your research questions, begin to outline or otherwise summarize how your data can be organized into your final product. Coding is only useful if it helps to push your project forward when you are unsure of how to proceed or need to organize your data for use in comparisons. Coding for the sake of coding everything is a waste of energy. The same for transcribing everything. Or interviewing everyone.

Listening is one of the core qualitative methods. While there are many considerations for conducting a study that only uses interviewing or focus groups, listening is even more useful as part of a project that uses multiple methods. The tools discussed in the next chapter, Looking, work synergistically with listening. Ethnographic participant observation improves the information that one has going into interviews, allows for longitudinal rapport with interview participants, and lets you triangulate the information gained through interviews with behaviors people actually do. Listening, though, will always be at the center of a qualitative project. Even while Looking, we must keep our ears open.

Recipes for Listening

1. Sampling Frames

Creating a sampling frame is quite simple once you have defined your population narrative. It becomes easy to predict your total estimated interviews from your axes of interest.

At its simplest, a sampling frame contains two axes. Here, as an example, we reconstruct a sampling frame that Petra Nordqvist (2012) likely used to guide her research study on lesbian couples negotiating conception (Table 5.2). Based on the information she provides, we can see her axes are Method of Conception and Class Status.

Select axes for your own study based on your population narrative. As you can see in Table 5.3, the realities of sample selection, recruitment, and theoretical saturation will leave you with totals that are different to a simplistic projection. It helps, though, to have an idea going in about the intersections between your categories.

Table 5.2

Sampling Frame	Reproductive Health Clinic	Self-Arranged Donor
Working Class	5 couples	5 couples
Middle Class	5 couples	5 couples

Table 5.3

Sampling Frame	Reproductive Health Clinic	Self-Arranged Donor	
Working Class	4 couples	4 Couples	33%
Middle Class	9 couples	8 Couples	66%
	52%	48%	

2. Interviewing Guides

An interview guide is a list of sample questions to help you navigate the interview and get the highest-quality, most relevant information possible.

An interview guide will look different depending on the type of interview you are planning. In this recipe, simply stop at the point corresponding to the level of specificity.

One begins developing an interview guide by brainstorming a list of topics. Typically, scholars pull the list of relevant topics from multiple sources such as previous literature, personal experience, prior interviews, and pilot studies. We recommend updating this list of overall topics after each interview, based on continuing analysis. When you've reached saturation on each topic, you're finished!

For an hour-long interview, shoot for around six to eight topics. If a topic appears to be producing longer responses than normal, you might have to arrange for follow-up interviews or decide to only address that topic with certain kinds of respondents.

This list of topics is an unstructured interview guide.

Ordering these topics will allow you to ask questions in ways that generate rapport and teach participants to answer in ways that are helpful to you. To that end, think in terms of a sensitivity curve. Your most sensitive, intimate, or difficult topics should be about two-thirds through the guide. Never just start off with, "So, tell me about the time when your father beat you."

Your first two topics should be questions that build rapport. Keep them light, but avoid demographic topics that will produce short, staccato answers. This stage of the interview teaches them to answer with longer responses. We recommend starting with a recent innocuous story, related to your project, of course: "Tell me about the last time you went to the Farmer's Market."

Topics three through five should build the intensity of the interview. Topic six is the climax of the interview. What are you most interested in? What are you most afraid of receiving as a "set response"?

Topics seven and eight ease the tension. You can't leave someone hanging in a vulnerable position. Instead, slowly return to everyday topics and issues. These topics are often best for "member-checking" questions that arise over the course of analysis.

After arranging your topics, create a few sample questions for each. You will rarely ask these questions exactly as written during an interview. Instead, they are there for back-up should you forget your next topic, the participant suddenly clams up, or you are unsure how to move the topic forward. When writing your sample questions, ask yourself these three questions about each one:

- Is this question open-ended? (Unlike this question's yes or no nature.)
- Which is better, a question that favors one response or one that lets participants make up their own minds? (Unlike how this question is leading.)
- What diction leverages esoteric knowledge derived from academic habitus? (Unlike this question's jargon.)

With these questions, you now have a semi-structured interview guide.

Lastly, write down the specific questions that you are going to ask, writing them down in such a way that anyone—either you or an assistant—could produce the same interview. Since you will be asking the questions as written on the page, you will need to build the principles of leveling into your guide. Vary the type of question—narrative, feeling, theory—and the time range—past, present, future plans, hypothetical. This ensures that you can triangulate responses within the interview, given that you will not be probing extensively.

This final list of questions is your structured interview guide.

3. Participant Recruitment

This recipe will focus on the basics of relational recruitment as described earlier in the chapter.

You will begin by brainstorming recruitment venues based on the cells in your sampling frame. Where would you find these people? For instance, in Nordqvist's study, she likely found couples that used health clinics through … health clinics! However, where would one find self-arranged donors? Internet forums or play groups that mothers frequent are possibilities. Working-class mothers, though, likely have less access or time to put into these groups. Remember to guard against unintended intervening issues in your selection of locations. Finding working-class mothers through government programs like WIC could add another issue that you would need to consider in your sample.

Once you have several options for each cell, recruit your "seed" participants from these organizations, locations, or lists. Try to shoot for two to three seeds per cell. These seed participants are the most difficult to recruit because they do not have a personal referral to vouch for your professionalism, enthusiasm, and congeniality.

From each of these participants, ask for referrals to "snowball" outwards through their social networks. As discussed in the chapter, we've found the most effective ways to increase diversity of referrals is to prompt the participant by describing the kinds of people you're looking for. You don't have to only recruit other people of the same cell as the participant! If Nordqvist was having difficulty recruiting working-class mothers with self-arranged donors, she likely prompted them with other kinds of participants. Try to find people who they believe would answer differently or who they don't know very well. Getting only a group of friends could skew your results.

A final warning: Don't get everyone from the same social organization, through the same seed, or even through the same method. The principle of multiplicity is at play: many different contexts come through each situation. Try to assess several.

4. Interviewing Exercise

This exercise involves two people role-playing an interview situation with a third person (or group) observing.

As the interviewer, your goal is to practice three key interview skills: developing probes on the fly, taking basic interview notes, and accepting silence.

The interviewee should answer naturally. Do not overly attempt to mimic a "bad interview."

Observers should comment on the interviewer's body language, question confidence, and missed probes.

Although virtually any questions could be used, we find these three produce a quick 10–15-minute interview that could be easily flipped:

- Tell me the story of the last time that you went on vacation or a trip.
- When you were young, what experiences did your family share of traveling to a different location away from your home?
- Describe your dream vacation for me.

5. The Note-taking Triangle

In this exercise, the goal is to reconstruct an interview from your notes alone and compare how those notes compare with the notes captured differently. This exercise works best in a group of three.

Each person will take a turn in each position.

The interviewer interviews the participant while the observer takes notes and handles the recorder. Because the experience is intense, keep the interviews short, perhaps five minutes. Each will reconstruct the interview afterwards. The interviewer has taken notes while she was distracted by interviewing. The observer has taken notes without that distraction. The participant should transcribe the interview. The exercise is over once everyone has taken a turn in each position.

Each position will hopefully reveal a different aspect. Some will be more faithful to the accuracy of words uttered. Some will be more faithful to the mood or tone of the experience.

What are situations in which each would be most appropriate?

6. An Interview Notes Template

We recreate the following three sections in our field notes.

Interview summary: A summary is your interview's abstract. In two to three sentences, what is this interview about? If you only had these summaries to go on, would you be able to turn back from writing a paper to find which interview holds relevant quotes?

Interview notes: We use the interview notes section for the interview's narrative, as partially captured by the notes we took during the interview. Since an interview begins before the beginning and finishes after it ends, this section also captures the information we were unable to write down in our notes at the time. How did this interview originate? Where did it occur? What happened during the interview itself? This is where you add embodiment, vocal tone, and other aspects that are invisible on the transcript.

Interview analysis: The interview analysis section contains your first attempt to synthesize this interview's importance. Why did you waste everyone's time and energy interviewing this person? This section records your hunches, the notes in the margins, the questions you asked connecting to other interviews, the quotes that remind you of that article you read last year. While you will memo more formally, connecting interviews together, these sections capture your thoughts while they are still fresh—often while you are still under the intoxicating adrenaline of an interview just completed.

7. Transcription

Should you transcribe? Many interviewers waste hours and precious research funds transcribing tapes that they never use. Full transcriptions of all your interviews might not be necessary if you are taking proper notes during the interview and properly debriefing yourself in analysis after the interview. In that case, you might only need to transcribe parts. Even if you wish to use analysis techniques that require transcription, it is overkill to code literally everything. Full transcriptions are an attempt by qualitative social scientists to reproduce the illusion of objectivity that positivism encourages. Use the "Interview

Summary" section of each of your interviews to designate what sections of an interview to transcribe.

After you've decided what to transcribe, you'll need to decide who will do it. Transcription is an extremely tiring, labor-intensive task. Outsourcing it to quality transcriptionists is expensive, easily the largest part of any small grant budget. Even if you have the funds to outsource, we recommend transcribing the first few interviews yourself. This closeness with the data will help in your analysis and speed the end of the project.

Transcribing yourself is made easier with the latest technology, which will already likely be outdated by the time this book is published. Many professional transcriptionists use foot pedals that let them stop and rewind the audio. Several computer programs can mimic this functionality with a hotkey. Consult trusted mentors for the current technological options.

Finding a transcriptionist balances price, quality, and time-investment. Professional transcriptionist firms can deliver high-quality transcripts and sometimes they are already cleared through your local IRB. As expected, they can be costly. At the other end, students, especially undergraduates, are willing to transcribe as part of a research assistantship experience. Quality issues can mean spending time spot-checking interviews, and a research experience that consists of transcription alone is impoverished. Freelance transcriptionists vary in these three factors. Ask around, you may find a good one. We usually use a mix of student assistants and freelancers who we've developed relationships with over the course of many projects.

These relationships can make your transcription more than a vehicle for coding or a dump for quotes. Skilled transcriptionists can add in extra-textual notes on emotion, tone, pauses, and laughing that can add life to the page when writing the final product. We recommend having you and your transcriptionist read Lynne M. MacLean, Mechthild Meyer and Alma Estable's article on improving transcription.[12]

8. Interview Analysis and Coding

Not everyone uses coding, and different types of coding exist. Use various tools to further your own theoretical development. They all are very helpful tools.

Open coding: Grounded Theory, and its various descendants, rely on open coding to stay close to the words and meanings of their participants. At its simplest, open coding involves going phrase by phrase, line by line, or paragraph by paragraph through your transcript and asking the question: What is going on here? Describe using action and verbs, avoiding jargon and academic terms that pull in outside concepts. These open codes can form the basis of future memos or be grouped to create categories that you can use in more intensive forms of coding.

Indexing: A middle-way kind of coding, indexing involves tagging sections of your transcript or data by topic. Indexing helps you to identify the kinds of data that you have available to you and the topics that your participants are discussing. One might index using open codes created by closely analyzing your transcripts, or you might index simply from your list of research questions.

Focused coding: The most advanced and complex form of coding, focused coding in traditional grounded theory takes open codes and categories created by your project and expands them to the entire corpus of your data. However, we take it to mean diligently applying a set of categories to your data that help you answer questions. For instance, in Jason's earlier work on coming out, he identified codes for three different strategies he found his participants using. After focused coding of his transcripts for these strategies, he was able to ask questions of the data: Did men and women use these strategies the same way? What were the contexts in which these strategies were being used? The focused coding then was not just about tagging areas for use as quotes in later works, it was also about analyzing and discovering new dimensions to his data.

9. A Note on Focus Groups

Everything and nothing is different about focus groups, depending on who you ask. Many focus groups essentially function as group interviews: a type of person recruited, an interview guide produced, analysis conducted on the transcript. However, focus groups have a specific flavor in many commercial and organizational settings. While we believe that the basics discussed in this chapter equally apply to focus groups, we recommend consulting a book specifically on focus groups if you are working with an organization, evaluating a policy, or creating a program.

© Matt Raboin

6
Looking
Ethnographic Observation

"Sure, I can hang." Jason told JJ—a Latino gay man who would become one of his **key participants**—the first night that he met him at Spin Nightclub, a gay bar in Chicago's Boystown neighborhood. They were the last words he remembers saying that night.

If there is one lesson in this chapter, it's this: Don't black out while conducting your ethnography.

JJ is a big man. At 6' 1", he had half of a foot and 150 pounds on Jason. He's a party animal, always ordering shots of Jameson's Irish whiskey or Jagermiester. When he asked Jason, "Can you hang?", the real question was thinly veiled. Can you hold your liquor well enough to hang out with me and my friends?

Jason knows the details of the rest of the night, even the parts that he doesn't remember, because the rules and skills of ethnographic observation are engrained. Walking home from the club that night—knowing that JJ had persuaded him to drink too much in an effort to prove he was one of the guys and not some pretentious academic—Jason took out his iPhone and spoke field notes into his recorder. Since he'd already been to Spin many times before with other participants, he focused on describing what was new: JJ and his friends. What were they wearing? What did they do? What were the topics of conversation? How did they react to the topic that Jason was interested in, sexual racism?

Jason didn't drink too much that night just for the hell of it. He did it because access is hard. (You may wonder about whether drinking is hard work, but it sure can be—especially if you aren't used to it. Mike was hungover for two days after trying to keep up with British farmworkers in the local pub one night. Not pleasant.) After all, Jason was asking people to allow him into some of the more intimate moments of their lives. He was trying to get a group of people who were in many ways different from himself—high-school educations or less, working-class jobs, different racial backgrounds, kids from previous straight relationships—to let him tag along, to maybe even become friends.[1]

He was asking to come backstage.

Erving Goffman examined social life through dramaturgical analysis, the metaphor of the theater.[2] As we go about our daily lives, so much of what we see around us is on the front stage. We show others a face to look good. At a restaurant, we talk to our dinner companions, mostly unaware of the server until she intrudes by asking for our order. She carries it out of the front stage and into the backstage of the kitchen. Her demeanor might completely change as she walks through the kitchen doors, perhaps talking about her tables with co-workers. If someone wants to know about restaurants, eating dinner on the front stage will only garner so much information. One must get backstage where the cooking is done—as the ethnographer Gary Alan Fine did in his book *Kitchens*.[3]

Looking—ethnographic participant observation—takes research beyond the words that attempt to explain but also cover up and excuse so much of what we do in everyday life. It's a crucial method of triangulation, to compare words to actions and to record aspects of situations that those enmeshed within them might not even notice. As they say, the fish is the last to discover water. By looking at both the front stage and the backstage of life, and comparing the multiple front and back stages that we move through, we can gain a better understanding of our chosen research problem. We can better understand our multilogical lives, in all their contextuality and intercontextuality.

Looking lets us see the structures that constrain action. It lets us observe the patterns of behavior, the scripts, that people follow—and sometimes deviate from, to everyone's surprise, even their own. Looking focuses on contextual understanding, appreciating contexts and intercontexts. One is not just observing people doing things, but also the places where they are doing them. Looking lets us see how people interact with the physicality of their locations, their embodiment within them, and the world of objects they manipulate. It is one thing to ask someone how to dance and another to watch them do it. Each method will give a different understanding of the action. Having learned to listen, now we must retrain our eyes.

Because we don't just open our eyes and see. Ethnographic looking is seeing a situation through another person's eyes, seeing how they understand the situation. Other methods also involve observation, but just as not every conversation is an interview, not all seeing is looking. Experimental observation involves watching. However, ethnographers watch differently. Ethnographic looking is active. It involves enmeshment. An experimental observer is more passive, taking down the plain view of what is happening. But a participant-observer engages herself within a situation and with others to gain what Weber, as we described in chapter 1, called subjective understanding and explanatory understanding of why people engage in the actions that they do. We need both understandings to interpret social contexts.

This *interpretive understanding*—understanding based on both subjective and explanatory understandings—is crucial to comprehending the singularity of the social world and how it can be extendable to other situations. Just as listening might force a researcher to confront some of her beliefs, looking forces a researcher to do uncomfortable things. The juxtaposition of the researcher between multiple social worlds—their own and the field—allows her to see the intercontextuality of the two. She is better aware of the multiple logics.

Ethnographies are necessarily case studies, seeking to understand more by focusing on less. (Sometimes less is more.) They seek the general within the specific in order to learn what is extendable through the singularity of a field setting. Ethnography is a form of "low-*n*" research because the number of participants might be very small. But by other metrics it is very high-*n*. Consider not just how many, but how long. Even an hour in the field can produce hundreds of ethnographic observations. Ethnography produces huge amounts of data, and yet there is always way, way more that could have been recorded. Human interaction is staggeringly complex, hugely multiple. It would be overwhelming to record all its dimensions! As we suggest throughout this book, attend to the case for as long as is necessary to understand it, no more.

Therefore, case selection is incredibly important. Many different cases might be good choices for a particular interest. However, choosing a case haphazardly or mainly for reasons of convenience can make your job much harder. A case should have the issues you are interested in forced to the surface, where they are most visible. You want a *black swan*.[4] (Or maybe a white whale!)

A black swan refers to a situation that stands out from the rest. An extreme case can make underground tensions more visible. The average might be more representative, but the black swan is a better representative for the process. This makes an ethnographer's job easier, so long as he is mindful of its singularity.

In these cases, taking a page from the extended case method (ECM) is helpful. As discussed in chapter 2, ECM uses a deductive approach to selecting cases. It seeks to extend a general theory of social life by finding a situation that is not well explained by the theory. By modifying the theory to work for that situation, you've expanded knowledge in that area. This deductive method forces you to consider the multiplicity and singularity of what you are trying to find because one must relate it to the overarching theory of interest.

One never just shows up and does whatever. You always start from somewhere, even if that is seldom where you end up. Even inductive methods like grounded theory start from somewhere, as Charmaz discusses in her constructivist revision.[5] Choosing deliberately, finding a black swan that obviously does not fit an existing explanation, forces you to choose a case from the perspective of your eventual audience.

Choosing a case is different from choosing a field site, although people tend to lump the two together. For instance, since Jason's case was gay neighborhoods, he chose Boystown in Chicago as his field site.[6] A case is a category of field sites that represent the problem under study. Mike's research in *Childerley* could have occurred in several different English rural villages, but he selected just one and got to know its specificities very well—the better to understand generalities.

Whether a field site is large or small, it is the area in which you circumscribe what you are going to be studying. It is the population narrative of "looking," just like the sampling frame was the population narrative of "listening." A field site might also grow or shrink over the course of research.

As a field researcher follows her leads, she might find herself in places she did not originally intend to be in. Be open about your boundaries and think about justifications—narrativity—for what you leave out or include.

A field site might also be field sites. The field does not have to be in one place. (Indeed, no one place is ever only one place—consider the diversity of spaces and people within it, all of whom will experience those many spaces at least a bit differently.) *Threads* by Jane Collins is an example of this kind of ***multi-sited ethnography***.[7] Her case—the industrial process of producing clothing—occurred in multiple steps across different factories and different industries using factories in different locations, a "commodity chain." Similarly, in your own multi-sited ethnography (should you choose that method), rather than examining a single space and the different threads that are coming through that space, you could follow a single thread of intercontextuality through multiple spaces. Multi-sited ethnography trades off a more detailed look at the singularity of a single space for reveling in the multiplicity of a process that moves through multiple contexts.

Alternatively, some ethnographies do the opposite and revel in the specificity of place. The classic "Chicago school" of ethnography represents this side. It wants to map many different aspects of a place to capture its context. One might call these ethnographies "multi-sided" in that they focus on the multiple logics within a single space. For instance, classic Chicago school ethnography *Black Metropolis* covers many different domains in Chicago's Bronzeville neighborhood, from the job market to religious worship.[8]

Today, we implore you to consider not only physical spaces but also the digital aspects of people's lives. Even people living in remote areas with no access to the internet now experience the effects of the digital world. Although some bracket this area off and call it "digital ethnography," it should just be called "ethnography." People use the online aspects of their lives to help constitute what goes on (or not) in their physical spaces. Consider including the digital aspects of your field site within your purview.

Getting In

Once you've narrowed down your case to a particular field site, the tricky issue of getting into the field arises. How do you get involved in situations in such a way that you are let into the backstage?

As Jason's story at the beginning of the chapter illustrated, access involves more than showing up, although that can go a long way to accustoming a scene to your presence. Many novice ethnographers are afraid of getting into "weird places" that they think will be difficult to access. They might be nervous because they fear the place is not for them because they do not share the identities of the people who frequent that scene, forgetting that a researcher will never be fully either insider or outsider. Ultimately, these fears come from the worry that they will ruin the space with their presence. They won't see what really happens.

The *Becker principle* is the notion that situations are so structured by social organization that a researcher's presence is not going to override the everyday rules of interaction.[9] Research participants are usually far more concerned about their own daily lives and the people they typically encounter in them than the passing presence of the ethnographer. Jason has done observations in the backrooms of leather bars, where people are having sex; they didn't stop because Jason was there. Mike is a Jewish man who has attended strongly anti-Semitic meetings of hard-right patriot groups; no one asked him about his religion.[10] Doug Maynard is a colleague of ours who uses conversation analysis of medical care, a method that often involves videotaping people during delicate and intimate moments: diagnosing autism, delivering a cancer diagnosis, soliciting a family member to donate a dead man's organs.[11] "You'd be surprised what people will let you videotape," he once told Jason. "They always eventually forget the camera."

The same is true for social situations. As long as you are respectful, there is a good chance that events will proceed normally. Once a group has seen you a few times, you will begin to blend. Don't inflate your ego. Yes, your positionality is central to your research—but it affects what you look for more than what you see people doing. You are not so important that others can't go on with their lives with you around.

However, this is not an excuse to overuse showing up. You have to have done your homework beforehand. And, of course, in some circumstances your particular presence does matter a lot. Which sometimes raises ethical issues. For example, is your presence going to be an invasion of a space that is intentionally fostered for a minority or stigmatized group of which you are not a member? These spaces are often the most studied by social scientists because "studying up" is harder than "studying down."

Elites have more ability to regulate what social access they permit, so social scientists sometimes take advantage of their privilege to force their way into minority spaces.

If this all sounds confusing—as though there's no right answer—it's because it is. Access in any situation is problematic. Access is a delicate balance of respect. Don't be rude. The most important question you can ask yourself is: Why do you want to access this space? Will your work be useful to the community? Will their They voice be present in the work?

Making use of a *key participant* is one answer, ensuring that you have a tour guide and someone who can provide a check on your desire to look at everything.[12] A key participant is someone who has persuasive leadership status within the social structure and networks within your field site. A key participant is the "gatekeeper" who can convince others to accept you. In Whyte's classic ethnography *Street Corner Society*, he identified these as people who, once he explained his work, would enable him to be unquestionably welcomed by others. Their word was good enough.

Frankly, a good key participant is also good at telling you "No." For example, in his ethnography *Farming for Us All*, Mike describes how he gave his manuscript to Dick Thompson, the founder of Practical Farmers of Iowa, the sustainable agriculture organization he was studying. Dick had been hugely helpful to Mike throughout the research, assisting with both access and interpretation. Dick read the manuscript and, when Mike met with him about it, made a key correction to Mike's analysis. Mike did not simply accept the point because Dick had said it. (The ethnographer should not take what respondents, even key participants, say at face value.) Rather, Dick convinced Mike he had missed something big. Mike completely rewrote the last chapter of his manuscript as a result. (Read it to find out why!)

Today, with the boom in research on communities, officials from organizations often act as key participants and their organizations become gatekeepers for you. However, use organizations cautiously, since they are also looking out for their own interests. In Jason's ethnography, *The Center on Halsted*, a multimillion-dollar community facility in Boystown, attempts to control information about itself and the community to ensure that the media presents the "correct" image of the LGBT community. Not surprisingly. There were many stories the previous year before Jason entered the field that presented "street youth" in the neighborhood as dangerous prostitutes and hoodlums who needed clearing. Key participants, like all people and organizations, have agendas, just as we researchers have agendas for our research. There will always be gatekeepers controlling access. It is our job as ethnographers to triangulate their They voices to better understand the multiple logics at play.

In the Field

By "looking" do we only mean looking at people? What do you look for? What are you looking at?

While your work may be highly focused, thinking from the perspective of a "total ethnography" is helpful. Much like the "leveling" discussed in Listening, we want to consider the situation's multiplicity to triangulate. We find it helpful to choose several aspects ahead of time—"What am I interested in tonight?"—rather than show up unprepared. As Peter DeVries says of writing, "I only write when I'm inspired, and I make sure I'm inspired every morning at 9 a.m." Similarly, choosing aspects doesn't close us off to the field's serendipity; it prepares us to be inspired by focusing our eye.

As social scientists we are interested in the connection between social structures and everyday interaction. Therefore, we suggest choosing both "micro" and a "macro" aspects during each observation—both contexts and intercontexts—but not too many.

Starting with the people themselves, who are they? How are they interacting? What does the space itself look like? Where are people arranged? How do they come and go? What activities are they engaging in?

What about the bigger, macro context? How do the political, economic, or racial fields come into play? "Macro" means different things to different researchers according to the context they are interested in. To one person, a city's political system might be "macro," while to another it will be a region's politics.

However, in thinking of the macro side, remember that ethnography seeks the general within the specific. You have to see those influences within the space you are observing. Your role as a researcher—the entire reason to bring the You voice into the conversation—is to be attentive to forces that individuals may not be fully aware of in the bustle of their everyday lives. You aren't a passive observer; you are an active watcher.

As a reminder, although ethnography places an emphasis on the observable, the tools of listening can be helpful by prompting participants to help you understand their environment. The ***contextual interview***, also called the "walk-along," works with the participant to help you see with their eyes. For instance, you might walk with someone through a neighborhood, discussing with them the places and people they see. You might never notice a group of people without their help. Working with someone at their job, describing how and what they are doing, is similar. Mike, in his book *Farming For Us All*, often used this technique. Whether it was riding along in the cab of a giant tractor or working up a sweat loading hay bales, working alongside these farmers helped Mike pay attention to the physical ways they revealed their identities as men and women through farming.

When you've seen all you need to see to write coherently about your project, it is time to start thinking about leaving the field. It can be a tricky prospect. How do you exit from the lives of people who have let you know them, sometimes very intimately? To a certain extent, you don't. Jason continued to live in his field site even after his main period of data collection ended. Both Mike and Jason still have friends and contacts among the people who were in the field—one of the pleasures of fieldwork scholarship we take up in the last chapter.

Consider though, that the Becker principle also applies in reverse. You are not so important to life that your absence will cause everything to break apart. Once you approach saturation, you have an obligation to not continue being a burden on this community and to bring their They voice out into the rest of the world through your writing.

Remembering to Remember

You can't rely on your memory. Notoriously unreliable, your memories change over time, reflecting new understandings and discarding "irrelevant" details that you may later find extremely relevant. Your *field notes* and *jottings* help you remember what happened in the field.

Field notes are descriptions of the scenes you encounter in your fieldwork, written in such a way that someone else can make sense of them. Jottings, on the other hand, are written for you to help you remember what happened out in the field and later use to write up field notes. Jottings are written as fast as possible. Field notes are more complete, reflective, and well written. Jottings can sometimes be taken during your participant observation. Field notes never are.

Entire books have been written about jottings. Ask 10 ethnographers and you'll have 11 opinions on the amount of detail these notes should capture, perhaps because no one has done an ethnography of what ethnographers actually do out in the field. Some ethnographers find ways to make it socially practical to take jottings while doing fieldwork. Others have scribble sessions at the first opportunity. And some ethnographers take no jottings at all. Instead, they immediately jump to field notes at the end of their session of observation. The geographer John Western is one ethnographer who often works this way.[13]

As is typical in this book, both of us tend to occupy the middle ground. We take brief notes during the situation of key phrases or events. We might draw a rough sketch or quickly capture a quote that will later help us remember to remember what has happened. Mike does this with a sheet of paper folded many times until it fits in the palm of his hand. Jason, a typical techie, uses his cell phone to capture quick notes, sometimes pretending that he is texting. (Mike is a grumpy hold-out and doesn't own a cell phone.) Others use a little reporter's spiral flip notebook. Some get their laptops or tablets out in quiet moments and type like demons.

Choose the level and means of jotting that seems appropriate to the situation, even if it makes you uncomfortable at first. The Becker principle applies similarly here to your writing and your presence. While people may ask you what you're writing down, it will quickly become commonplace. Many ethnographers notice that people sometimes reference the recording device and beckon them to write down what they are doing, indicating that they are playing to the camera, so to speak.

Turning those jottings into field notes is one of the most time-consuming and important parts of ethnographic work. Field notes are the data that you're going to be returning to throughout your work. They are the way to remember what you've done. Neither your hazy memory nor your hasty jottings will be decipherable a year later when you return to a particular scene. Here is a key principle of ethnography: *Write it down.* "If you're not writing it down, you're just hanging out," a colleague told Jason once.

What do you put in your field notes? A dry rendition of what happened is not going to strike at the core of events as they unfolded. You're not a passive observer; you're an active looker. We use the **three EMs** to remember what to remember: *emplacement*, *embodiment*, and *emotion*.

Emplacement refers to the physicality of the objects and location that surround you. For every new space that you're in, you should write a set of field notes that describe that space and how people use it. For larger areas, such as whole neighborhoods or schools, it can be helpful to have a table of contents, referencing where descriptions of each part can be found. Consider as well creating visual references, like maps, for your areas. These can be invaluable references for keeping your descriptions consistent while writing your final product.

Embodiment is the people within the space. What are they doing? More than that, you need to remember what they were doing with their bodies. If you merely write down their key phrases, then you should have conducted an interview. Then at least the Listening you did would have been more accurate. Take advantage of what Looking allows—data from your other senses. In this way, ethnography is the most erotic social scientific method, relying as it does on your visual, olfactory, and tactile senses to make sense of the social world.

Finally, take care to represent the emotions of those present. The emotional content of their actions represent moments that are breaching the social dryness of everyday life. These are the grabbing moments that others will remember when discussing your work. Emotions make more vivid prose. Remembering them will help you remember so much more, and tack better between subjective and explanatory understanding.

Overall, your goal is to balance what the famous field worker Clifford Geertz called ***thick description*** with ongoing analysis.[14] Thick description is almost at the level of fiction in its generosity of detail about a situation. Thick description reveals something new. Forcing yourself to describe a situation in such detail that someone who has never seen anything resembling it might be able to understand what it is like—will give you a fresh perspective. Seize these moments of insight for memos, especially when they seem unrelated to your topic. Quite a few insights that Jason thought were unrelated to his book topic came together later to be facets of a much larger process. These came only from thickly describing the dancing of individuals on a dance floor, the nuance of a business meeting about building a hotel, the physical differences between two bars. You don't take it all in while you are taking it all in.

However, thick description can too easily become a thicket. It can be too boring. Remember that it is the iterative process between description and theoretical analytical memos that move your work forward. Thick description is a tool. It should be used to advance your work, not as a crutch for procrastination. We know of many ethnographers—novice and expert alike—who have spent so long endlessly describing, collecting event after event, that they end up like so many hoarders, alone in an empty house, with numerous possessions but no one to talk to.

It can also be incapacitating. Fieldwork can easily produce such vast quantities of data that the researcher is overwhelmed and doesn't know where to start—if they decide to wait until the end of the project before they begin to interpret and analyze. In addition, fieldwork data doesn't easily reduce into neat tables, as we discussed in chapter 4. It confronts you with reams of text and hours and hours recordings. It's real-time, or nearly real-time, data. Even with modern computer search tools it can be hard to find and assemble the instances from your work that you need to feel confident about a conclusion. (There is no search tool to find phrases in your audio files.)

So we can't emphasize enough the importance of analyzing as you go along, iteratively, both to guide your theoretical sampling and to avoid having to deal with piles and piles of stuff lying in confusing mounds on your desk and filling up folder after folder with unsorted material on your hard disk. Don't wait until you come back from your fieldwork. Please, please don't.

Think of it this way: Imagine you are translating a live speech from English to isiXhosa, the language of the amaQwathi people of South Africa, a situation in which Mike often finds himself with his current research. Do you wait until the English speaker has gone on for five minutes or even ten before asking her to pause so you can translate for the non-English-speaking audience? No. You'll barely remember even the outlines of what was said five or ten minutes ago. Instead, you translate in small bits—maybe even one sentence at a time—as the speech goes along.

Because ultimately, ethnography is an act of translation. You're attempting to translate a social world for two audiences. For an outsider audience—the We voice of research—you're making a world intelligible to people who have never been there and might know nothing about it. Thick description and ethnographic insight help to translate this knowledge into a form that outsiders are going to be able to understand. But don't wait until the end before you begin.

You also want to be able to translate this world for those living in it—the They voice of research. In this way, the positionality and positive bias of your outsider status are helpful. You want to give people a new way of looking, enable them to see things that are around them in a different way. To help people who might be in these situations with new ways of seeing their lives in all their contextuality and intercontextuality.

You have to be able to do both to have a true multilogical ethnography. Otherwise, you're engaging in a more positivist extraction of data for the outside world. Doing both helps achieve a balance between these two voices. However, there are times when and reasons why you don't want a balance. For example, you may want a project that deliberately privileges the They voice that has been so often neglected in scientific research. For certain topics and problems, you want to go beyond Looking and Listening and truly participate.

Recipes for Looking

1. Access Canvass

This book's constant refrain is, "There is too much to look at." A field is not a singular thing. Even after you've chosen a field site, based on a case, for theoretical reasons, you still must narrow down the areas within that field that you are interested in.

However, we often don't know what we have to choose from. If you're at loss—and even if you're familiar with your field site—doing some canvassing can be helpful.

Canvassing, in electioneering terms, involves going door to door in an area, talking to voters about a candidate or an issue to convince them to vote for your candidate. This generally involves listening to voters, hearing their concerns, and answering questions about why they would not want to vote your way. We want you to canvass your field for participation.

Walk—if feasible, and common amongst your participants—through your area(s). Walk into businesses. Knock on a few doors. Find a few community meetings and attend them. You are not asking people to participate in your study. You don't even have a study yet! You are listening for potential access issues, assessing general willingness for an ethnographer to exist in the space, and gauging the depth and variety of groups in the area.

For instance, say you've chosen to do an ethnography of accounting firms. You've narrowed this down within that category to, specifically, corporate accounting firms within Texas, perhaps because of unique state regulations that relate to your research questions. Before you cold-call the partners at a Dallas firm—and likely get turned down—go to an accounting conference. Attend a meeting of the local professional guild. Find a few bars where employees go after hours. Arrange for coffee with a few partners at firms around the state.

All of these activities will generate issues with access for you to solve. All of them provide opportunities to gain background information for your initial inquires. All of these will lead you to contacts that you can leverage when you finally settle on a specific firm. Don't wait until you've already "started."

2. JOTTINGS 3X3

We've discussed a number of ways to do jottings and some different kinds of situations where they might be appropriate. This exercise, best done with a partner, allows you to experiment with different styles.

Table 6.1 below shows the possibilities. Choose a method from each column. We've marked the three that fit together best. Select your way of looking and way of recording and observe a situation with your partner. After you have turned your jottings into field notes, compare.

Ways of Looking

A Fly on the Wall is the distant observer. Sit in an area and interact as little as possible. Best use: Observing change in an area over time.

Table 6.1

		Ways of Looking		
		Fly on the Wall	Casual On-Looker	Immersive
Ways of Recording	Transcriptionist	x		
	Selective		x	
	Memorizer			x

A casual onlooker interacts, but not consistently. If you've ever sat in a bar for a longish time, talking with different people over the course of the night, then you've been a casual onlooker. Best use: Introducing yourself to scenes that reoccur many times or are stable.

Immersive experiences are those you most need to remember to remember. Whether dancing with a group of participants or working the line in a factory—when you are immersed in an experience—field notes are the difference between research and hanging out.

Ways of Recording

The transcriptionist makes every effort to record everything that they see. Knowing this is impossible, the transcriptionist attempts to record a single kind of observation in that moment. The transcriptionist is not necessarily writing this down. Duneier's always-on tape recorder while he worked the bookstands in *Sidewalk* was this style.

Selective jottings capture key quotes and small notations to jog your memory later once you are writing field notes. This style of jottings is perhaps the most common.

The memorizer does not take jottings in the traditional sense. Instead, they dump their memory onto a tape recorder or notepad after they have left the situation. This memory dump is not field notes. Rather, it acts as the basis of formal field notes written at a later time.

3. Training the Eye

People can be the least interesting part of fieldwork. Social scientists want to comment on the social, of course, but the places people move through and the objects they interact with are important elements of their social lives. Places were designed by people. Businesses arrange themselves to best sell their goods. Objects, food, clothing—all reflect social tastes.

To train your eye, use a camera. Looking through the lens and composing your shots focuses your eye on these nonperson elements of ethnography. Return to the brainstorming list for Multiplicity in chapter 2 and spend a day in the field taking pictures. Take at least 20 pictures. Ten of these pictures should reflect a theme on the Multiplicity list on p. 32. Use the other ten to reflect emerging ideas for your topic. While "Life Span" or "Economic Systems" might seem lofty concepts disconnected from the particulars of your field, connecting the two through image will train you to see the general in the specific.

This kind of visual ethnography is also engaging for readers, and we will return to it in our chapter on writing.

4. Field Notes: A Template

Field notes can be incredibly time-consuming. They are useful, but don't let them get out of control. Like a gas, writing them will expand into the time allotted. The following template can help, making sure that you've written at least something about a variety of topics and that you've pushed forward towards analysis.

Entering the field: How did you get there? Who did you arrive with?

Exiting the field: When did you leave? Why? What plans do you have to see these people or experience this event again?

New participants descriptions: How and why did you meet any new people during this field excursion? Describe what they look like, their personality and their relationships to others you already know.

New place descriptions: Where did you go and why? Describe your surroundings, including a physical description and a description of the groups present.

Timeline: For future reference, write a short synopsis of events.

Areas 1 and 2: It helps to have a few areas of interest before each event; write at least a few sentences about each one.

Epic write-up: Now you've written about the above topics, you're ready to spend your remaining time going into more detail about the events you witnessed. Do not start at the beginning! Like an epic, begin with the action, what you consider the climax of the event. You want to focus your analytic and descriptive talents on this climax. Otherwise, you may find yourself always describing arriving and then losing energy to finish your notes properly when the action starts.

For more on writing field notes, see the book by Emerson and colleagues, aptly titled *Writing Ethnographic Fieldnotes.*[15]

5. Analysis: Writing Forward

As we move on into less positivistic and less traditional styles of data collection, analysis becomes less formalistic.

In addition to tools like coding, we recommend writing forward. You can always collect more data and social life is infinitely complex. We repeat this line throughout this book. Analyze towards the goal of communication. Have you answered the questions you set out asking? Can you communicate these answers to others? Have you anticipated likely criticisms? What form will you communicate these insights? Who is your We, the audience of your work?

Only by regularly checking in with your project can you answer these questions.

We reproduce below a check-in that Jason wrote 13 months into his ethnography, *Boystown*. You can see some of the chapters that eventually appeared in the book begin to form. Since he was conducting this research for his dissertation, he speculates on the questions for the three articles he would need to present to his dissertation committee.

> Update on the Project Narrative
> I have three papers that I'm going to be writing for the dissertation:
>
> 1. The cost of assimilation (see the latest memo on this from reading Pais South and crowder 2012): This argues that we should look at the intersection between residential segregation and sexuality, the influences of both gays gentrifying an area are clear, but what are the influences and consequences of the late stage gentrification? What are the consequences for the sexual field, and its interplay with the racial field, when you have straight sexual mores taken into the bars and clubs

2. Sexual Racism in Augmented Reality: This is the paper that I gave a presentation on: The changes that I have described above have come along at a time when augmented reality is becoming a reality. The ethnosexual field adjusts. This paper describes how racial dynamics exist both offline and online, but that they look decidedly differently in the online sphere, with consequences for sexual racism. Given augmented reality, they are going to be going both ways
3. The Sexual Ethnographer: The methods piece that I'm writing and I did a morning pages memo on several days ago: There is a long history of taboo around sexuality in ethnography. This paper chronicles a part of that history and then argues that in an ethnography on sexuality, you see some of these factors more saliently than you do in other ethnographies, but that they are influential either way: 1) Sexual Stratification (desirability of the ethnographer as a sexual partner) 2. The sexual field (relative role of sexuality in the place the ethnographer is working, including assumptions on the part of potential participants) 3. The Ethnographer's Sexuality (Influence of being single/partnered on ethnography, the sexual identity of the ethnographer, going places differently)

weeds contribute little to
of animals, and open grazing
are usually full of them. In
grazing, the animals can freely
tastiest plants. So any
of them spoke up, a
"But you're counting the
she said. "Well, of course,"
replied. "But that's not a
Because there are
no weeds a MIRG pasture." Her
with. Weed
chemicals
was initi
But the
od point,
A questio
fields.
than
these

© Matt Raboin

7
Participating
Research as Practice

"Mike, they're a little concerned about something back there," she whispered.

Mike caught the eye of one of the farmers sitting on the wagon behind the tractor and watching his hurried conversation with Alex, a graduate student at the University of Wisconsin. Mike could sense what she meant. The air hung with more than humidity. There was an unsettled feeling, even as the farmers appeared to be listening to the agronomist standing before them in the field, explaining the trial he had run the previous summer. The farmers were trying to be polite, but plainly did not agree with the agronomist.

These were graziers—farmers who raise livestock mostly on pasture grass, relying little, if at all, on grain, and using a special technique called "management intensive rotational grazing," or MIRG. Agroecologists applaud the approach. Instead of packing animals into a muddy feedlot and shoveling corn at them or letting animals wander willy-nilly through a big field and graze unevenly, MIRG rotates animals through a series of small paddocks, allowing farmers to keep the grass at a medium height where it is the healthiest, fastest growing, and most nutritious. MIRG saves the soil, limits water pollution, provides wildlife habitats, and gives livestock a nice life with no need for the "maintenance dose" of antibiotics feedlots use. Plus MIRG is highly productive—maybe even as productive, acre for acre, as feeding livestock corn.

MIRG seemed like a great thing to encourage, Mike and his student Alex thought. But university researchers had historically been pretty skeptical and hadn't promoted it much. Plus they didn't really understand what the graziers were doing. It sounded to Mike and Alex like a great opportunity for *participatory research*—research where expert knowledge comes together with the local knowledge people have from their everyday lives, each helping guide the research process. Even more, it seemed a great opportunity for *action research*—research that seeks to make an improvement in a problem people face in their daily lives, rather than merely studying the problem. Put the two together and you have what is sometimes called *participatory action research*, or PAR.

So Mike and Alex worked with the agronomists to organize a "field day" to discuss their research trials with the graziers. It wasn't going well, though. The agronomists were doing almost all the talking. Before lunch, they even presented PowerPoint talks in the barn. Plus the agronomists were making a claim that the graziers thought was flat-out wrong: that MIRG isn't any more productive than unmanaged grazing in big open fields. Randy, the agronomist in the field, was explaining his methods for comparing MIRG with open grazing. The graziers, of course, did not want to believe his results. But they could also see a big hole in the methodology. They didn't feel they could challenge the professor, however, so they were grumbling among themselves.

"Um, Randy," I interrupted. "I think you've got a question back there."

The flow paused. Graziers exchanged looks. Then one of them spoke up, a woman grazier. "But you're counting the weeds," she said.

"Well, of course," Randy replied.

"But that's not a fair comparison. Because there are almost no weeds in a MIRG pasture."

Her point was technical, dead-on, and really important for interpreting Randy's results. He had been comparing the productivity of MIRG and open grazing by periodically clipping all the growing biomass in test plots—grass and weeds alike. But weeds contribute little to the nutrition of animals, and open grazing pastures are usually full of them. In open grazing, the animals can freely reach for the tastiest plants. So any weeds grow and spread. Plus, with MIRG the graziers move the animals before they chew the grass down to the soil. Consequently, weeds have little chance to get established. Weed control without chemicals is one of MIRG's biggest advantages, according to advocates. And yet the researchers were treating all biomass the same, weeds and grasses alike. The graziers felt Randy and his colleagues should only count what animals actually like to eat and that is nutritious.

Randy was initially defensive, understandably. But then he agreed that it was a good point, one he hadn't thought of. A question still remained in the graziers' minds, though: Would Randy do anything about it? Would he listen to them and actually change the research?[1]

Research with People

At Iowa State University, where Mike used to teach, the motto on the school seal is "Science with practice." Researchers sometimes joke that the motto means that, with a little more practice, they might actually achieve better science. But the motto really means that the purpose of a US "land grant" university is to do useful research, not science for science's sake. You start out from the world and all its problems, not your discipline and all its problems.

Participatory research shares this motivation, but carries it a step further. We might call its goal "practice with science." Practitioners become researchers, while remaining practitioners. The research subjects help choose the subject of the research. They may also work with researchers to collect and analyze the data. In some forms of participatory research, the role of researchers is more to help the practitioners conduct research than the other way around. Or possibly outside researchers may not be involved at all. This breaking down of the traditional barrier between who is the researcher and who the participant can also move in the other direction: researchers becoming participants, studying themselves through techniques such as *autoethnography*. But whether the movement is in the direction of practitioners becoming researchers or researchers becoming practitioners, the basic goal is the same: To better connect the They voice and the You voice.

After a slow start, participatory research has recently become something of a small revolution in the academe. Take sociology, our own field. The phrase first appears in the database *Sociological Abstracts* in the 1970s, with four entries. It shows up 36 times for the 1980s and 91 times for the

1990s. It rockets to more than double, with 253 entries for the 2000s. At the time of writing it continues to double, with 225 entries just for 2010 through the middle of 2014.[2] If we add the phrases "action research" and "participatory action research" to the search, all numbers basically triple. For example, for just 2010 to the middle of 2014 there are 872 hits.[3] That's a lot of studies.

And why not? It makes sense to combine the eyes of those embedded in a social context with the eyes of the "stranger," as we phrased it in earlier chapters. And it makes sense to combine their voices in guiding the conduct of research. It's, well, a more multilogical way—the research strength that this book seeks to encourage.

After all, society spends a lot of money supporting academic researchers through tuition, grants, and direct government support. The idea had long been, though, that specialists should judge the quality and importance of any research project, as they know best the right methods to use and their positions free them from political bias. But this means the academe polices itself. Some worry that science winds up being unaccountable to those who are paying most of the bills: the public. Much research consequently focuses on disciplinary concerns that may thrill specialists but often seem pretty far removed from any practical application. And others worry that self-policing by the academe can also mean too much accountability to special interests: the corporations which increasingly support academic research, especially in the natural sciences. Because of academic freedom, the public has little voice to complain about corporate influence in research. In other words, conducting research without participation is no guarantee of protection from bias.

As our opening vignette suggests, keeping participants from having an input into the conduct of research is no guarantee of protection from inaccuracy either. Academic researchers often have a great comparative perspective and excellent theoretical insights. But they may miss crucial matters that people local to a situation know and live every day. To put it in the terms we have been using in this book, practitioners are usually strong in their understanding of contextuality and weaker in their understanding of intercontextuality. Experts? Usually the other way round.

Plus, both natural scientists and social scientists have a brilliant array of measurement techniques. They can assess factors that local people may not even realize exist in their situation. But are the scientists measuring the most significant factors? Like the difference between the production of grass versus weeds? Sometimes yes. And maybe sometimes not.

The social anthropologist Jeff Bentley makes a helpful distinction between the *conspicuousness* of a dynamic and the *importance* of a dynamic.[4] Expert knowledge is great at sussing out the inconspicuous, especially those matters that one needs special tools to ascertain. But experts are often too unfamiliar with a specific situation to recognize what is most important. Experts can be so overwhelmed by the multiplicity involved in any case or setting that they miss much of what really moves things, especially if they are personally unfamiliar with that setting. Local knowledge's strengths flip the polarity. Practitioners local to a situation can readily point out a lot of important factors, especially easy-to-see ones, like weeds in a field—factors that may seem obvious, but whose significance only becomes clear when one has a good handle on the context. But are practitioners going to have the tools and time to carefully measure these factors—for example, to compare the overall biomass of weeds versus grass in a field across a whole growing season?

In short, experts are good at assessing the inconspicuous but often weak at assessing importance. Practitioners typically have a good idea of importance, but do not have the tools for measuring what is hard to see.

Moreover, the emotional coolness and distance that researchers generally feel they need to maintain in order to be "objective" often gets in the way of gathering needed evidence. As Randy Stoecker, a longtime advocate of participatory research, notes, "the creation of emotional distance in fact [has] often made the research less accurate. Because the researcher refused to build trust with the research subject, the research subject withheld information from the researcher, essentially spoiling the results."[5]

So how about figuring out ways to draw on the strengths of both expert and local knowledge, overcoming the weaknesses of both in the process? Why not work together, building trust both ways, participant with researcher and researcher with participant?

Indeed. But it may seem a bit strange, especially at first. The contours of participatory research often lead to some unfamiliar shapes of scholarly endeavor. For one thing, the usual boundaries between social science research and natural science research often collapse. We chose our opening vignette for this chapter in part to highlight this collapse. As you were reading the vignette, you may have wondered why a study of grazing techniques would involve social scientists. But to gain the value of multiple perspectives we need a good understanding of the social processes by which multiple logics can come together—especially across a power divide, such as outside expert versus local practitioner.

Another unfamiliar contour of participatory research is the way it scrambles the line we usually draw between qualitative and quantitative research. Sometimes the data gathered during participatory research is entirely quantitative—another reason we chose our opening vignette. That study of MIRG was numbers, numbers, numbers, pumped through high level statistical analysis. Or participatory research may gather only qualitative data. Or a mixture of both. What makes a study participatory is not the means of gathering data, but the process that guides the research.

Central to that process—or any process—is how you handle power relations. It takes more than bringing experts and practitioners together to do participatory research. You have to engage them in a common project in which each values what the other has to offer. Done well, experts come to appreciate practitioners as the experts of practice, and practitioners come to appreciate experts as practitioners of expertise. Done even better, participants understand themselves as having what our colleague Loka Ashwood calls *grounded knowledge*—knowledge grounded in one's own experience but potentially also in others' grounded knowledge or experience, just as one place on the landscape ultimately connects to all others.[6]

Processes of Participation

So do you try to eliminate power differentials in order to conduct participatory research? Good luck. People have their lives, their needs, and their positions. While you (and we) may hope that a participatory approach to research will contribute to ameliorating inequalities, you have to work within the world as it is. But what you can do is help participants—whether experts or practitioners, and including yourself—recognize their positionality. You can encourage the embrace of *reflexivity:* the appreciation, as C. Wright Mills famously put it, of one's own "history and biography and the relations between the two within society."[7] Call it self-awareness in pursuit of other-awareness.

Some early work in participatory research, however, did see its task as eliminating power relations in research. Concerned that their own agendas would unduly shape or pollute the research, scholars proposed a variety of procedures for ensuring "bottom-up" control of what would be researched and how. They had reason to be concerned. Even if scholars conduct their work using the most careful and objective scientific methods, the work will be biased in two important ways: what Mike elsewhere calls the problem of *selection* and the problem of *reflection*.[8] The problem of selection is the question of what research will be done and what research will not be done. Scholars do not have unlimited time and funds. They must choose what and what not to study. The selection effect quickly becomes a question of who the research is *for* and what are the power structures that shape those interests. The problem of reflection is the question of what categories researchers use in understanding their work. If the categories are their own, then the results may amount to little more than their own reflection in the mirror. Research becomes me-search. The reflection effect, then, quickly becomes a matter of who conducts the research and what are the social structures that give them their position and authority and ways of looking at the world.

The unavoidability of selection and reflection effects raises troubling ethical issues. So early advocates of participatory research tried to devise an array of best practices to ensure that those being researched have major input and control at every stage of the research, from problem identification through to analysis and implementation and evaluation of any prescriptions for social action that come out of a project. Scholars came up with typologies and scales to indicate how truly participatory a project was, and sets of procedures to move research higher up the "ladder of participation."[9] But two difficulties emerged. First, participatory researchers often seemed to manifest a kind of professional guilt over the power that comes with college degrees and good paying jobs at universities and other research organizations. So concerned were they to eliminate the effects of this power that participatory researchers had a hard time admitting the effects were still there, leading critics to accuse participatory researchers of being "naïve about the complexity of power and power relations" and of "mythologizing" what actually goes on in participatory research.[10] Second, the procedures early participatory researchers advocated tended to be formal and rule-bound. The goal was to make sure that those with greater social power did not dominate decision-making. But formal and rule-bound procedures actually advantage those with social power, as they typically have the most experience and ease navigating them.[11] The very people such procedures aim to welcome often find them alienating, and disengage from the research process.

What to do? First off, it seems unhelpful to pretend that power can be escaped in any research process. We don't inspire the participation of experts by telling them that they need to set their own interests and positions aside and pay attention only to the interests of others in conducting the research. Nor does it build harmonious research relations to suggest to practitioners that their interests are the only ones that matter. Yes, experts are the ones with the authority to publish scholarly work and gain credibility for its results. They have a lot of power there, and there is great potential for selection and reflection effects to shape research outcomes. But they are also the ones who have to publish scholarly work in order to keep their jobs and advance their careers. Asking them to squelch those realities does not encourage reflexivity and mutual understanding. It encourages delusion, and it raises the potential for conflict and hidden power moves because people feel they cannot be frank about their situations and needs.

Second off, it seems equally unhelpful to expect there to be one right way, or even four or five right ways, to handle power in research relations. Lives and situations are too varied for that. We cannot start out participatory research by establishing common situations, knowledge, expectations, and needs. Indeed, the existence of a lack of those commonalities is the whole reason to attempt participatory research to begin with.

In short, participatory research is pretty messy stuff. But that's OK, for out of that messiness comes much of the creative and liberatory potential of participatory research to bring multiple logics together into new ways of understanding the world.

Once again, consider that scene in the pasture with which we opened the chapter. Randy and the other natural scientists involved in the study of MIRG could hardly have begun the field day with a clunkier social move: sitting farmers down on folding chairs in a dark barn for PowerPoint lectures on numerical research results. Randy and his colleagues weren't trying to hide anything. They were communicating research results in the way they had been trained to do, and they were genuinely hoping for some useful input from the farmers—although they were, as yet, a bit skeptical that they would get much. The farmers hardly said a word. Things got a little better, though, when we broke out the braised beef sandwiches for lunch, made with beef raised by one of the farmers. (It was not a vegetarian crowd.) People milled around, chatting, joking, crossing a few social boundaries. The stuffy and hierarchical mood began to lift. It lifted even more when we loaded the group, researchers and farmers together, onto a wagon with hay-bale seats, everyone a bit tumbled together. Hierarchy reasserted itself when Randy got off the wagon to lecture again, this time out in the field. But once crossed, social boundaries are more easily crossed again. And so a challenge filtered its way up, but also across, the lines of power, from farmer to graduate student to a professor who was not on stage to a professor who was.

We individually interviewed everyone involved afterwards, and one of the farmers said: "I think that comment almost wasn't made that day. I think some of us sometimes hesitate to jump out and say what seems obvious to us but is not on the table. I think maybe we need to do a better job of, if there's something we see, say something!"[12]

She was clearly feeling that her views would be welcome, because, in fact, Randy did change his experimental design to reflect what the farmers had earlier pointed out about the weeds—with results that demonstrated MIRG's greater productivity. Yes, the farmers were motivated in part because of their own interests in promoting MIRG as an alternative to grain-feeding cattle or open grazing. For his part, Randy was motivated by his interest in maintaining professional credibility. So there were power dynamics on both sides. But this change in knowledge happened both in spite of power and because of power, power that nonetheless did not stand in the way of people's productive engagement—though it nearly did.

Our point is the importance of what Alex, Mike, Randy, and a couple of other colleagues came to call, with a bit of a smile, *maculate conceptions*. There is no perfect, immaculate way to conduct participatory research. It's pretty much always a mess, as we noted above. But that mess can give birth (conception as creation) to new ideas (conception as concepts) that emerge from the mutual dialogue of many logics and many purposes and situations (con-ception, from the Latin for together-taking action). Maculate conceptions. The trick is to find in that mess a way to build everyone's reflexive awareness of their own positioning, their own grounding in the landscape of human experience, and thus their eagerness to hear from others about their different groundings.

By the end of the MIRG project, the participants were well along toward that reflexive awareness. As one of the natural scientists said, "I have learned a tremendous amount just by seeing what [graziers] do, understanding the challenges that they have, and realizing that they have a lot more to think about when they're managing their farm than [my research interests]."[13]

And at the second field day, a year later, there were no PowerPoint presentations. No one felt the need. Instead, everyone in the barn sat around one big square of tables pushed together—not a perfect circle, maybe, but much better than rows facing a projector screen. The mood was relaxed and open, welcoming mutual grounding of knowledge. One of the researchers mentioned that he wished he could do more with the great points and questions that the farmers were raising, and how frustrated he was that his career constraints prevented him from doing so.

"Well, isn't that partly because of our general ignorance of the research process and what's involved in it?" one farmer replied.

"But the farming community needs to understand your limitations and your needs and what you can and cannot do for us," added another farmer.[14]

Through increased reflexive awareness of themselves and each other, they were learning about the creative contradiction at the heart of participatory research: differences in power, perspective, needs, and interests are both a great challenge and a great opportunity.

Forms of Participatory Research

Participatory research may seem a novel idea. Top journals in the social sciences still rarely include extensive discussion of it or articles that highlight their use of participatory techniques. But versions of participatory research have long been part of professional research practice, even if researchers generally think they shouldn't say much about it publicly.

Take the working habits of Calvin Beale, senior demographer with the US Department of Agriculture until his death in 2008 at the age of 85, still at work after 55 years of charting—literally, for he made lots of charts—the trends of rural life. He was the great sage of rural statistics, famous for being the first to notice that the US's rural population, long in decline, rebounded in the last quarter of the 20th century. Beale actually identified the trend before it first showed up in the 1970 census. Colleagues scoffed because the numbers didn't yet show it. But Beale's motto was,"You can't know what's going on in the country from behind a desk in Washington."[15] Two or three times a year he would head out into the countryside, driving fast (apparently he had something of a lead foot) to cover a lot of landscape, but frequently stopping to talk with locals at bars, restaurants, churches, and coffee shops. He is reported to have visited over 2500 of the US's 3141 counties during his lifetime.[16] And in the 1960s he noticed a lot of new homes going up and old ones being refurbished and heard from local people about their communities growing in numbers even as main streets were being boarded up, due to competition from big-box retail.

Or, to take an example from the natural sciences, consider the discovery that glaciation used to cover vast areas of North America and Europe. The 19th-century geologist Louis Agassiz first proposed the notion of the Ice Age in the scientific literature in 1837. But the germ of the idea was suggested in 1815 by a Swiss farmer to a skeptical geologist hiking past his farm. The farmer, Jean-Pierre Perraudin, told the geologist, Jean de Charpentier, that it looked to him like the glacier up the valley from his farm had once stretched much further down. De Charpentier published an article about the idea, but it didn't attract much notice.[17] Agassiz hiked through the region in the 1830s, talking to lots more farmers about the odd out-of-place stones they had seen, the sand left where no river could deposit it, the scratch-marks on rocks, concluded it must be true, and published his famous article connecting the evidence in Switzerland with similar evidence elsewhere in Northern Europe and North America.[18]

But these examples, valuable as their insights have been, must be recognized as only very weakly participatory. The defining characteristic of participatory research is that participants help guide the research process, or even control it entirely. Neither Beale nor Agassiz conducted their research in that more deeply collaborative way. They sought the impressions of local people, and possibly also their advice, but did not grant them much (if any) power over the process of the research.

We should make the same distinction with "participant observation," which we discussed in the previous chapter. The term participant observation is sometimes confused with participatory research. One might easily, and appropriately, do both at the same time. One might use the techniques of participant observation to gain access to situations and get kinds of evidence that might otherwise be invisible to research. That's why Loïc Wacquant, a White man born in France, joined a Black boxing club in Chicago.[19] That's why Nancy Scheper-Hughes, an American anthropologist, moved into a mud-walled hut in a Brazilian favela.[20] That's why Barbara Myerhoff spent two years working with the members of a Jewish center for the elderly in Venice, California.[21] That's why Jason went drinking at Spin. (Really!) But this kind of up-close-and-personal research does not necessarily entail involving the subjects of the research with guiding the research.

At least not in an official way. As we mentioned in the previous chapter, participant observation work often hinges on the insights of "key participants." For Wacquant, it was DeeDee, head coach at the gym. For Myerhoff, it was Shmuel and Rebekah, two of the center's members. Key participants do more than consent to interviews and observation. They put in a lot of time helping the researcher gain access, extending trust in the researcher's intentions to others in the setting. They give the researcher background context about the important strands of multiplicity in the study site. They correct the researcher when he or she has made a social faux pas or an analytic error. Typically, key participants become deeply invested in the outcome and success of the research. Sometimes quite a lot of guiding goes on.

Take Mitchell Duneier's ethnography *Sidewalk*, his study of Black men who try to gain a livelihood from New York's sidewalk life, panhandling, selling goods, scavenging from dumpsters and recycling bins. Hakim Hasan, a street vendor selling what he termed "Black books," was absolutely crucial for the success of Duneier's award-winning study, giving advice, making contacts, providing vital background observations about street life, and critiquing Duneier's interpretations. Presenting your results to those in the field study, and getting their feedback, is a form of participatory research called *member checks*. Most qualitative fieldwork studies can incorporate member checks, at least in some form. We strongly recommend the practice.

But Duneier did even more. He was so impressed with Hasan's critiques that he arranged for the University of California-Santa Barbara, where Duneier was teaching at the time, to pay Hasan to co-teach a seminar with him on "The Life of the Street and the Life of the Mind in Black America." And at the end of the book he published an Afterword by Hasan—who had a college degree, even though he was a street vendor—giving Hasan direct interpretive control in the published work.[22]

Duneier also afforded some interpretive control for some of his research participants who did not have high levels of writing skills. Mike once invited Duneier to give a university lecture on his book, and Duneier brought along Ishmael, one of the men in the book, who had little formal schooling.[23] Duneier used the honorarium to buy bus tickets for the two of them from New York out to the Midwest. After Duneier finished his presentation, Ishmael took the lectern for 20 minutes of stunning eloquence, without a single note.

Like most scholars, Duneier hoped his research would have practical impact, and it did, challenging the "broken windows" theory of crime which demonized street people as the start of a slippery slope of neighborhood decline, resulting in their receiving much abuse from authorities. But let us suppose your research focuses on people's immediate needs, rather than trying to reform public policy. Let us suppose you are working to improve livelihoods and health in a poor rural community in, say, South Africa, where Mike is currently involved, working on several projects in the high grasslands of the Eastern Cape Province. Even though South Africa is Africa's richest country and even though apartheid officially ended in 1994, the legacy of inequality continues, combined with one of the highest AIDS/HIV rates in the world. How does someone from far away help?

Probably not by trying to turn the patterns of village life there into something like Mike's own pattern of life. It's just not going to work. But what else does someone like Mike really know about?

Increasingly, experts and specialists embrace *participatory development*, a form of participatory action research, to handle this common problem of development work. Perhaps you know of a more nutritious crop that will improve people's diets. Or a valuable handicraft that people can sell. Or a technique for improving the quality of local water. There may be very good reasons why local people aren't doing those things already. Maybe they don't like the taste. Maybe people are rightly concerned that profits from the handicraft would be controlled by local elites. Maybe the water improvement technique is too expensive and requires maintenance skills and tools they don't have. Or maybe they are simply tired of well-meaning rich people telling them they know how to solve their problems, and then returning to their lives of privilege, guilt assuaged. Participatory development says, wait a minute. Let's empower people to be involved in solving their own problems, with outsiders contributing resources, technical assistance, and a few ideas to the dialogue of multiple logics. Not only are participatory solutions likely to better fit people's needs and circumstances. If people feel they are part of coming up with an intervention in their lives, they are far more likely to buy into it and to be committed to making it work.

Or maybe experts can help make it possible for local people to do research on their own. Instead of locking our knowledge away in obscure language in obscure journals, researchers can give local people the tools to conduct excellent research with little or no assistance. Especially in developed countries, lots of people are highly trained professionals in their own special area, and those skills are more transferable to another area, with just a bit of help, than specialists often like to think. Maybe a community wants to dispute the claim by some local company that their facility does not pollute, or isn't causing the local spike in cancer rates, or does not discriminate against women in their hiring and promotion practices. Someone sends some emails to professors at the nearby university, asking if they can come in and gather and analyze the data to make a case. Maybe they're lucky and someone actually responds, eager to help. And maybe that person actually attends a few community meetings. But then that person just sort of fades away, caught up in administration, teaching, and the need for publishable work which advances their career. It happens. All the time. So how about if experts put some work into making the methods and results of research widely available—on the web, perhaps, or through workshops and field days—so communities can do their own good science? This approach to participatory research is sometimes called *community-based research* or *community-based participatory research*. Many successful social movements have been based on it, from the Love Canal Homeowners Association to the Detroit Community-Academic Urban Research Center to the Practical Farmers of Iowa.[24]

These are all forms of what has come to be called *citizen science*—ways of bringing participants into the research process as knowledgeable people capable of making careful, sophisticated analyses of their own circumstances. We've only been scratching at the surface of the great outpouring of creative work on devising new forms of citizen science. Indeed, every participatory study encounters different circumstances and different needs and seems to come up with at least slightly different ideas about how to welcome the engagement of expertise and practice. It is definitely the kind of thing where you want to develop qualitative cooking skills rather than simply following a recipe devised independently of your research situation. Maybe think about it this way. Participatory research is not a method in itself but a method for carrying out methods: a reflexive awareness of everyone's awareness.

Participating with Your Self: Autoethnography

Including your own awareness. Increasingly, scholars have been trying out ways of treating their own experiences as legitimate evidence. Want access to people's deepest thoughts and most intimate encounters? Try using your own. Try being your own ethnographic subject through *autoethnography*.

Unquestionably, autoethnography remains far more controversial than citizen science forms of participatory research. We are more comfortable with the idea of people as researchers than with the idea of researchers as people. The objectivist legacy of science remains strong as the foundation of legitimation for the scientific enterprise—an enterprise that costs a lot of public money, as we noted earlier. In the face of debates about "junk science," "science for hire," and various forms of "denialism" from climate change to gun control, academics are understandably cautious about methodologies that might be seen as undermining the vital contribution of scholarship to public life. Whether or not one agrees with objectivism, the argument goes, it remains the academe's main cultural support.

We don't want to get into a long discussion about the philosophy and politics of science here. We'll do a bit of that in the final chapter, anyway.

Instead, we'll make a more pragmatic point. Like citizen science forms of participatory research, autoethnography is actually quite common and ordinary in scholarly work—especially qualitative fieldwork. We're usually just uncomfortable being open about it or about labeling it as such when we do it openly.

But is it wrong to consider researchers' own reactions to a situation as evidence about that situation? Creative non-fiction writers use their own reactions all the time in their writing, and their work often has huge impact—at least in terms of book sales. Take the work of the ecologist and poet Sandra Steingraber. A "Rachel Carson for our time," as she is often described, Steingraber's books about environmental pollution constantly reference her personal experiences. In *Living Downstream* she talks extensively about her own brush with bladder cancer. In *Having Faith* she considers the toxins in her own body during her pregnancy with her daughter Faith. In *Raising Elijah* she considers the challenges of raising Faith and her son Elijah in a world threatened by climate change and the ubiquity of toxins. Her experiences lend credibility to her passions, encouraging the reader to take seriously the numerous shocking studies that she reports and that readers might otherwise wave aside.

Or take Rebecca Skloot's accounts of her own emotions and personal history in *The Immortal Life of Henrietta Lacks*, her book about the poor Black woman whose cancer cells were taken from her, without her knowledge, shortly before she died, and sold as the HeLa cell line for innumerable cancer studies while her family languished in poverty. Here's how her book begins:

> There's a photo on my wall of a woman I've never met, its left corner torn and patched with tape … . Her real name is Henrietta Lacks. I've spent years staring at that photo, wondering what kind of life she led, what happened to her children, and what she'd think about cells from her cervix living on forever—bought, sold, packaged, and shipped by the trillions to laboratories around the world … . I'm pretty sure that she—like most of us—would be shocked to hear that there are trillions more of her cells growing in laboratories now than there ever were in her body.[25]

We meet Henrietta Lacks in this introduction, but we also meet Rebecca Skloot, and we learn about her passions and moral values. Details such as how Skloot has Lacks's picture on her wall and how the left corner of the photo is "torn and patched with tape" would never make it into a conventional social scientific research article. Journal editors and reviewers would find these passages irrelevant and subjective. And even if they were accepted as relevant, what proof other than Skloot's word do we have that there really is such a photo on her wall? But to the reader of creative nonfiction, these details build identification with the subject, both through accepting Skloot's eyes as the reader's own eyes and through gaining a bit of the passion that led Skloot to keep that photo on her wall so long, even after it was torn and patched.

This kind of personal and introspective writing is becoming increasingly common in qualitative fieldwork, especially outside the confines of journal articles. University presses now welcome it—as long as there isn't too much of it. But how much is too much? Scholars still very much disagree about this. But pretty much everyone agrees on one point: The old narrative practices of the "god's eye view"—passive constructions, never using the first person voice, no mention of the researcher as a person—make for stultifying writing. If you want your work to be read, make it readable. If you think your topic is interesting, don't make it boring.

We do recommend, however, that qualitative researchers be careful about being self-indulgent. Most likely, people aren't reading your work to learn about *you*, cool as you are. But readers welcome learning about the subject of your work through your experiences, in all their vividness. Take these passages from Jason's forthcoming book about Chicago's gay village, *Boystown*, where he describes how women, both straight and lesbian, often participate in "man hole" events (often to the annoyance of gay men).

> "Woo! To the birthday girl!" I toasted, hitting the glass against the bar before slinging back a shot of Jameson at Hydrate's Man Hole night. Each of the five straight White women in front of me took theirs. One grimaced, only managing to shoot about half of it. As the warmth hit my stomach, I thought to myself, this place is not quite as Sam had described it.

> [...]
> The next time I was at Man Hole night, women were there too. Two shirtless lesbians made out in the corner, one cupping the other's bare breast as she pushed her against the wall. They blended into the scene. The space was packed, crowded with men grinding on each other in time to the music, most wearing leather and other fetish gear. Austin and I drank our whiskey-gingers while talking with a friend wearing a full suit of rubber gear. His boyfriend stood behind him, dressed similarly except the dog collar and leash.
>
> On that night, I saw a tall Iowa boy, chunky and muscular, get his dick sucked in the dance floor's back corner. He had a leather harness wrapped around his chest before extending down over his stomach to attach to a leather cock-ring. I tried to avoid looking, lest I make them feel self-conscious. An ethnographer's job is hard.

It's vivid. It's sexy. It's funny. And there's a whole lot of Jason. But imagine if Jason tried to take himself out of these scenes. In an effort to be objective he would have to fictionalize. Because he was there and he did have personal reactions to what he was seeing—reactions that, among other things, dictated where he allowed himself to go and even where he turned his head, shaping the evidence he was able to gather. And because he gives us a window into his own feelings and decisions, we're able to judge whether we find him a trustworthy and reliable witness. To put it in objectivist terms, we're able to take into account the kind of measuring instrument he is, giving us a better sense of what seems accurate and what he might have missed. By being less scientific, Jason is more scientific. And we're able to go into settings along with Jason that we might otherwise never go into. We learn about Jason in order to learn about his subject, not to learn about Jason as a subject (although Jason actually is pretty cool, says Mike).

Jason doesn't label his presence in these scenes as autoethnography. Nor does Mitch Duneier, Nancy Scheper-Hughes, Loïc Wacquant, or Barbara Myerhoff. More controversy has surrounded work that explicitly calls itself autoethnography, such as Carolyn Ellis's extraordinary study of her emotional reactions to the progressive illness and eventual death of her partner.[26] If her PhD were in English, probably no one would have been troubled by her methodology and her writing. But Ellis's PhD is in sociology, and she mainly publishes as a sociologist in the sociological literature. Autoethnographic methods and reporting techniques such as introspective journal entries, vignettes, switching between narrative voices, critical incident analysis, auto-interviews, and even imagined interviews cross the line for many scholars. It's still not the kind of thing that makes it into the *American Journal of Sociology*.

Yet it can win Academy Awards. Although she doesn't call it autoethnography—the term hadn't yet been invented—Myerhoff's *Number Our Days* makes extensive use of the method. Especially striking are her imagined interviews with Shmuel after he died. Here's a short sample:

> "Shmuel, I can't help but feel somewhat sad that your death was so little noticed while Jacob's [another member of the Center's community] was given so much attention. You deserved more honor and gratitude."
>
> "Now you are talking like one of the bobbes [the grandmothers]," he answered. "Haven't you learned from me that one thing has nothing to do with the other? If I would be like him, who would be like me?"[27]

During her research at the Center, Myerhoff collaborated with director Lynne Littman on a documentary about her project. Myerhoff is a central figure in the film. And it won the 1976 Academy Award for Documentary Short Subject. That doesn't happen to your ordinary scientific research project.

Autoethnography is also the main method of one of the most widely acclaimed works ever written by a sociologist, *The Souls of Black Folk*, by W. E. B. Du Bois. He didn't use the term either, writing a century before someone coined it. But you know he was writing about his own experience of race in American when in 1903 he wrote one of the most widely cited passages in the sociological literature:

> It is a peculiar sensation, this double-consciousness, this sense of always looking at one's self through the eyes of others, of measuring

> one's soul by the tape of a world that looks on in amused contempt and pity. One ever feels his two-ness,—an American, a Negro; two souls, two thoughts, two unreconciled strivings; two warring ideals in one dark body, whose dogged strength alone keeps it from being torn asunder.[28]

So maybe we need to lighten up and recognize we researchers are human too—that we have a double-consciousness of our own as practitioners and experts. Or maybe a triple-consciousness, for participatory research actually does more than connect the They voice and the You voice. It also brings them together with the We voice, uniting better with the audience for scholarship with vivid, intimate, and practically significant work.

It's all forms of Us.

Recipes for Participating

1. Collaborative Autoethnography

Interactive ethnography, community autoethnography, co-constructed ethnography, deliberative autoethnography, and more. It has had many names. One of the lessons of this chapter has been that participating breaks down the barrier between They, You, and We. You can be a participant. They can be researchers. We can all be collaboratively present.

Therefore, why shouldn't a group use autoethnographic techniques?

We used collaborative autoethnography with our colleague Gina Spitz in a paper examining the role of power in Erving Goffman's presentation of self.[29] Mike and Jason had each been involved in a class activity, and then Gina and Mike were involved in the same activity the following year. Through weekly meetings and examining video recordings of both events, the three of us were able to deliberate on and compare our experiences, especially our inner emotional states during awkward moments captured on tape.

Similarly, participatory action research could use collaborative autoethnography by teaching autoethnographic techniques to participants, who then analyze their own experiences. Those analyses can be the data themselves, or presented together to triangulate on a shared experience.

2. Contestability in Autoethnography

Like the rest of qualitative research, one of the biggest questions with autoethnography is: How do we know that you are telling the truth? This is a topic that we've dealt with exhaustively throughout this book. However, when listening, looking, or doing participatory action research, there are objective references that researchers use to build contestability. What do you have as an autoethnographer? We have to take your word that this event happened or you felt a particular way. This doesn't mean that contestability is out of reach for autoethnography. You become more scientific by being less scientific. Autoethnography's strengths lie in the tools of emotional recall and translating, bringing the singularity of an event to life through your positionality. By providing specific details about an event and limiting your theoretical generalizations, readers increasingly trust that you are accurately reporting events and feelings. Autoethnography tends to attract criticism relating to verifiability, but in this respect it is no different from any of the other ways of knowing that we have discussed.

However, there is an ethical consideration unique to autoethnography that the other methods do not share. While it is easy to assume that "auto" means "one," you are actually not the only person you are writing about in an autoethnography. We are seeing a scene from your viewpoint, your positionality, but social experience is relational. If you are writing about fox-hunting with your father, your experience of the hunt is not yours alone. What details are you going to include about your father's actions?

Jason wrestled with this issue when he wrote an essay about coming out to his father as gay. Although the essay was meant to demonstrate the inadequacy of the idea of coming out as a one-time event, he couldn't tell a story about coming out without describing *to whom* he was coming out. Jason's dad still hasn't read this essay. When Jason asked him why, when writing this book, he answered, "Well, our relationship is good now. I didn't want to bring up old fights or feelings."

When writing an autoethnography, it is never just you that you are writing about. You have to consider the consequences of your writing on your intimate partners, friends, and family. Your work will be read by others, sometimes by the people you are writing about. Choose your words carefully.

3. Participating with …

This might seem obvious, but a participatory project involves actually participating *with* people and communities. It might not always be obvious, though, who those people are. Communities, groups, ethnicities, identities, and stakeholders are made up of many parts. They aren't monolithic entities of which one can say, "Oh, I worked with the neighborhood." Who are the neighborhood and why are they participating with you?

Let's tackle these questions systematically.

First, why do *you* want to do participatory work? What are your motives for wanting to do participatory research, especially participatory action research?

Second, how are you going to determine who to work with? There are two general options for where to start. You can choose a group first, allowing you to involve them in the choice of topic. Alternatively, you can choose a topic and then search for a group or community that might be interested in working on that topic.

Third, who *within* that community are you going to work with? Let's say you are working with a neighborhood advocacy group on local violence. Are you going to work with that group to the exclusion of others? Are you going to attempt to bring others from the neighborhood who are not involved in that group into the meetings? Community groups don't speak for everyone. You have to understand who it is they are speaking for, and then decide whether there are other voices you want to bring into the conversation.

Fourth, even narrower, groups are composed of individuals, with their own agendas and interests, just like you. Why are they interested in working with you on this project? Who stands to benefit from their collaboration? Will there be people left out of the research, action, or proposed solution because of who you collaborated with?

Answering these four levels of questions when you are proposing a participatory action project helps you be specific and understand the positionality of the researchers that you will be bringing into the project.

4. The Nobel Savage

Namely, who is a participant? As we discussed in "Participating with … ," communities are not monolithic. Working with one community group in an area means not working with another community group. Everyone has their own agenda, including you. Think through who you are participating with before embarking on any action.

Because the question "For whom?" must always be asked of the "action" of PAR. Well-meaning outsiders regularly come into communities seeking to help the downtrodden. They impose their will and their dollars and then fly off to the next underprivileged area before they gain any understanding. This is one of the areas where PAR is favored. It attempts to involve and turn over decision-making about solutions to the people who will be affected by them.

However, turning over that power to other groups doesn't allow the researcher to abdicate all ethical responsibility for the solution. We call this fallacy the "Nobel savage" problem. Early anthropology often perpetuated the stereotype of the noble savage, the racist primitive simplicity of those "less civilized" than the European and American researchers. Today, especially in PAR, researchers are less likely to assume that the community is less knowledgable and more that they have all of the answers. They see them as Nobel savages, experts and savants by virtue of their otherness. Doing PAR is a careful negotiation, a study in power relations. You are an expert, with knowledge of past missteps and misdirections. They are also experts, with knowledge of their own community.

A prime example of this tension is to be found in data collection efforts by participants in PAR. As a researcher, it is still your responsibility to train participants in the ethical ways to collect data: confidentiality, respect, preventing coercion.

However, don't let these ethical power dilemmas deter you from attempting PAR. Despite the potential for harm—the researcher running roughshod or participants favoring their own interests—participatory action research is still one of our best ways of dealing with the ethical dilemmas that we have discussed in previous chapters.

5. The Research Cycle

Let's break down the idea of "participating" even further. There are many parts to "research," and the group you are collaborating with could be involved with any part of it. For our purposes here, let's assume you are working with a community group in a neighborhood, seeking to understanding the influence of neighborhood context on their children's education.

Question and Problem Selection

Who wants to be involved in defining the parameters of the question? Someone must choose the topic and also define and operationalize the problem and case.

Pros: Collaboratively choosing the topic and defining the case means that the group is going to choose something that is relevant to their own lives. In this case, a topic they care about, their children's educational outcomes.

Cons: They might also choose something you have little or no interest in. If you're a researcher on agriculture (like Mike) or sexuality (like Jason), a chosen education topic might be outside of your professional area. This is a good time to interrogate yourself, though. Why are you uninterested? Is it a lack of relevance for you, or are your skills elsewhere? Would this topic be seen as a radical departure from your research program? These questions will help you negotiate the boundaries of the project with the group.

Method

How will you answer your questions? As we've discussed throughout this book, that depends on your problem. Not all questions can be answered with just any method. However, there are a range of ways to approach an answer. Which ones will be used?

Pros: Involving the community in this process can be very rewarding, especially if they are going to be involved in the data collection. The community group might have considerations you can't know about, just as the farmers knew that cutting all the plants, rather than measuring grass alone, would lead to a biased answer. In this example, perhaps the group knows that personal interviews might be hard to solicit in their community. Or perhaps that survey researchers are mistrusted because of past community trauma.

Cons: Many of us are specialists in particular methods, which might make it hard for you if they choose a method of data collection and analysis with which you are unfamiliar. Do you have the time to learn new methods? (Hint: you might have more time for and experience with picking up new methods or skills than they do!).

Data Collection

Who will be collecting the data? Are community members going to assist? Are they going to be the only ones collecting data or will you be collecting data concurrently?

Pros: Just as there are issues of positionality that you experience when you interview or conduct fieldwork, community members have their own positionality vis-à-vis other members of their community. Their insider status might make interviewing more personal or their fieldwork more autoethnographic, or give their surveys a higher response rate.

Cons: Data collection is time-consuming. Training new interviewers, ethnographers, or surveyors takes time. Involving the community at this stage could significantly increase the length of the project.

Analysis

Who will "answer" the questions that you developed together? Will the process be iterative, with you as researcher doing constant member checks with the group? Are you going to conduct the analysis on your own and then present the answer to the group? Will you lead the group through the analytical stages solely as a group?

Pro: Doing analysis together can help break down the barriers between scientist and practitioner. Community members might be able to help suss out key details that are worth focusing on, able to translate their own experience.

Con: Revealing the researcher behind the curtain might actually make the group less trusting of the results. The allure of the objectivity of science is strong. Also, people might not be sufficiently familiar with the methods of analysis in your field to help.

Presentation of Results

Who will work on the presentation of the results or the development of an action? How are the results of the study going to be presented: presentations, scientific articles, books, websites?

Pros: Let's be honest, involving them looks really good. It helps the project's contestability within participatory action research to include participants in the presentation of the data. In presentations, people can ask them directly about their involvement in the process, verifying your methods. Also, the group would likely prioritize areas that communicate the results to audiences that matter to them, audiences that you might not know how to target or be trained in writing for.

Cons: You also have to consider yourself and your own needs in the presentation of data, needs that are likely to be less salient for the community group. While you might need peer-reviewed journal articles for tenure, those articles might not make any difference to the community. You want to negotiate a balance.

If all these pro/con lists seem to lean towards the pros, it's because, although there are many cons to consider, they can usually be overcome or they might reveal more about you and your positionality than they do about the community.

However, you have to choose when to be involved and when not to be involved, for several reasons. First, the community might not want to be involved in everything. That's why they brought you in! You are the expert from the university who's here to help them, not burden them with trivial decisions to assuage your guilt because this is your job. One group might want to be involved in the data collection because they want it to double as community outreach to their members and also want to learn new skills. Another might send you away to do that work yourself because they are busy, uninterested, or unfamiliar with the method.

Second, you might not want them involved in everything, not only for the reasons discussed above but also because having them involved at every step of the way is going to be enormously time-consuming. Qualitative fieldwork is already time-consuming: having to quit and consult every step of the way might not be ideal for your situation, with things like the academic job market, tenure decisions, and publishing deadlines ahead of you.

In all cases, it's a negotiation. You aren't their puppet researcher and they aren't your passive subjects. Building the project together throughout the research cycle will help make sure the work that is involved helps everyone.

6. Member Checking

There are several kinds of member checks, although researchers tend to be slippery about which one they used. Here, we've organized them from least to most participatory.

- The "Am I right?": The purpose of this check is to reflect your research back to participants. It is useful for discovering disconfirming cases, because participants can think of examples of when your work is wrong in their lives. However, it is easy for it to turn into a one-way street, since telling someone they are wrong is hard to do in conversation.
- The Check-in: The purpose of this check is to follow up with participants later in the research cycle. They can help you determine whether you interpreted their words correctly or give you updates on stories that they told you previously.
- The Phase Two: This check is part of iterative analysis, asking participants themselves to help you interpret their actions and those of others.

We use each of these kinds of member checks in different parts of research. Determining how to incorporate the feedback that you get during member checking is delicate. Just because someone disagrees with you doesn't make them right and you wrong. You've conducted research in this area for a reason and with skill. You didn't pull your analysis or theory out of nowhere. However, there are no outliers in qualitative research. You need to think through why this person might disagree with your analysis. A negative member check becomes a great disconfirming case. For this reason, member checks are very useful as a way of noting exceptions, places where your theory and data have limits. Others use member checks as an alternative commentary within the presentation of the work. Duneier, for instance, included in his book *Sidewalk* an essay by Hakim, who reflected on the work from his own position. However, he also used member checks with Hakim as part of iterative analysis. He originally "finished" his book with a set of results different to those in the published version. Hakim challenged his interpretation, which led him to collect new data and expand his views.

Member checking isn't for the "end" of research. It is part of the research process itself.

7. ADDING ACTION

"What do you plan to *do* with your research?", someone asked Jason at a conference. It is a hard question. What do you plan to do?

Largely, the answer is an issue of extendability. What other circumstances will find your work useful?

But action research attempts to go beyond traditional extendability. It gives back to the people who gave you data, esteem, and a project that brings you material dividends.

Adding action isn't about presenting in interesting places or to new audiences. It is about using the work to shape a solution to a problem that materially helps the lives of participants or communities that contributed to the project.

It isn't going to be easy. Adding action might be difficult because of local actors and organizations that control the area. Take Jason's work in Boystown. A community center called The Center on Halsted and a neighborhood group called the Northhalsted Business Alliance exercise tight control over the projects that happen in Boystown. If they aren't working with you, you can be frozen out of doing something with certain groups, such as business owners or disadvantaged queer youth.

How can you actually do it, though? You might be looking at this page, wondering why there isn't an exercise you can do to think through how to develop a project. More than any other part of participatory methods, action has to come from people themselves.

8. CITIZEN SCIENCE

You are an expert in your area. However, you have plenty of other work to do. You can't do all of the projects on your topic. There is too much multiplicity in every context! You could, though, make your methods or knowledge available for others to use. Give someone a fish, that person eats for day. Teach someone to fish, that person eats for a lifetime, so the saying goes. There are two ways to make your work publicly available.

Public data

You can make your data open for secondary analysis. We often associate secondary analysis with quantitative data, because large datasets are difficult and expensive to put together. To make the most use of their time and money, the data is specifically designed to be shared. While less common with qualitative work, it is still possible.

The most major issue is that public data use has to be worked out ahead of time with IRBs and participants. One way to do it is the approach that oral history archives use. Participants sign disclosures that make their interviews confidential until their death. Obviously, this is something that involves thinking ahead. Another approach is to make the data anonymous in such a way that others will not be able to identify your participants—but this is harder than you think. So much of our stories involve others.

Public methods

Another way of enabling citizen science is to help non-experts become experts using your methods. There are many ways to learn methods—this book among them—but could you develop something that teaches people specifically how to study your topic?

9. Emotional Recall

Emotional recall, or as Carolyn Ellis calls it, "heartful autoethnography,"[30] is the process of plumbing the depths of your emotional responses to an event. Writing intensively and personally about how something made you feel can help reveal some of the dynamics of the event to you. Emotional recall is one of the best tools of autoethnography because we only truly have access to our own inner emotional lives. Emotion is under-discussed in research because it is hard to empirically verify. We can see someone's actions. It can be hard to say why someone is crying unless we know quite a bit about their context.

As an example, take the last social event that you attended. Write two different short essays.

In the first, write a paragraph or two only describing the actions of others. What happened?

In the second, write those same events but include your emotions. It may help to visualize the events. How did you enter the room? How were you feeling when you got to the event? Did the warm smile of a friend make you happy as you arrived? How did seeing that person that annoys you make you feel?

Just as we discussed "levels" in Listening, accessing different levels within your experience, including your emotional experience, is key for autoethnography.

10. TRANSLATING

Many forms of autoethnography (see Ellis 2009) are based in a critical pedagogy, seeking to disrupt the often colonial and powerful "researchers" with indigenous, post-colonial, and marginalized voices. Explaining an experience that others have not had is difficult and involves what feminist Marjorie Devault called "translating." Devault (1990: 101) argued that, "since the words available often do not fit, women learn to 'translate' when they talk about their experiences."

In that case, Devault was talking about translating participants' experiences through your own, to help give voice to things that are said incompletely because our language itself is an expression of power. As a participant yourself, your autoethnography is an act of translation. How can you explain something to an outsider who may not have had these experiences?

Through metaphor.

Working with a partner, think of an epiphany, a turning point or other key life experience. Choose one that is connected to a part of yourself that you consider to be a key identity that the other person does not share. The goal of this exercise is *translation*, after all.

Your goal in your conversation is to find a common life experience that you can use as a metaphor to bridge your different social positions. Your similarities become a guidebook for navigating the unfamiliar terrain of your epiphany. They aren't supposed to be an exact match. Rather, explaining the similarities and differences can help someone who never experienced an event to gain insight.

For instance, Jason has no children, while Mike is a father of two. How is Mike to translate for Jason, who has not had this experience, what it was like to teach his daughter to play music? How can he communicate the joys and frustrations? The investment in getting it right, the pressure to not be too pressing? There are a number of analogies that Mike could use. An obvious one—Jason is a son with a father—is inadequate. It doesn't capture the teaching aspect. Mike could use an experience they both share—mentoring students in a classroom—to bridge that gap.

What can you translate for others?

Ways of Telling

All of this is not to say that
there aren't artistic choices
within academic work. We
certainly think that there are.
Some of the most interesting
work blends genre, capturing
multiple
those are only the most
artists. All writing is an art
Your selection of a cover to
your work. The way that you
blend quotes into your
of theory. Your font. These
are also artistic choices. Use
of the elements available to
to reinforce your words.

© Matt Raboin

8
THE MULTILOGICS OF WRITING

There is no "writing up" phase of research.

Writing is present from the very beginning of the project. Designing it. Discussing it with collaborators. Comparing your ideas with earlier work.

Research is writing.

Writing focuses our mind. To put a sentence together, and then that sentence together with another, requires us to use logic—if nothing else, the logic of language. Indeed, the etymological root of the word logic is *logos*, ancient Greek for "word" and "speech." As we like to tell our students, writing is thinking.

We write our thoughts to convey ideas to an audience. Even if no one sees your writing—like Jason's daily journal that he uses to warm up before work—you are writing for the audience of your future self. You are checking your thoughts against the logic or logics you expect your audience to use. Thinking is dialogue.

Yet, while we ought to consider the logics of others constantly throughout designing and conducting our research, we are often most attuned to them when we are seeking to convey what we've found. We shouldn't wait that long. Dialogue is research.

Put it all together and we can see the central place of writing in the multilogics of field research. Research is writing, writing is thinking, thinking is dialogue, and dialogue is research.

There are many wonderful books on writing. For the sociological, there's Howard S. Becker's *Writing for Social Scientists.* All academics should read *Writing Your Journal Article in 12 Weeks* by Wendy Belcher.

The methodical look to Eviatar Zerubavel's *The Clockwork Muse*. The creative seek inspiration from Steven Pressfield's *The War of Art*, and Julia Cameron's *The Artist's Way* speaks to the more spiritual among us.

This chapter does not attempt to replicate the fine advice these and other sources give—such as the famous dictum, "Just damn write it." (OK, we did just replicate that bit.) Instead, this chapter delves into the unceasing writing that occurs throughout a project and looks at how it connects us to the minds and words of others. We consider both *multilogical writing* and *writing multilogically*—the theory and the practice of multilogical communication.

Multilogical Writing

Begin by thinking about the end. While you will be writing constantly throughout the process of working on a project, your project generally ends by presenting something to others. That's your goal. You want to tell others about your work. So think about the end from the beginning. The We of research should guide many of the decisions that you make all along the way—so much so that this chapter could well have gone at the front of the book. The design of your project, the academic literature that you engage with, and the point at which you consider your research done all depend on whom you consider your audience to be and what you consider their demands are. The logic—really the logics, plural—of the We is in constant dialogue with the You, as the You in turn dialogues with the They.

Let's consider two ways the They shapes your research throughout your project: narrativity and contestability. How will you convey the inevitable partiality of research? The question of narrativity. How will you encourage people to regard your work as worth engaging, despite—and maybe even because of—your partiality? The question of contestability. Earlier, in chapter 3, we presented narrativity as a dimension of the You voice, and in chapter 4 we presented contestability as an issue of the We voice. Here we endeavor to show how narrativity and contestability can connect, thereby connecting all three voices.

Venue

How will you write? Different presentations of your data are better suited to different audiences. The format and venue is your first writing decision, because it influences your decisions for narrativity and contestability. An academic audience has different expectations to a popular audience. For example, a popular audience might need some concepts explained in plainer terms and will also want your writing to be entertaining. After all, they don't have to read what you write (unless they are students assigned your work in a course!). If it's dull, they'll pick up something else. A professional academic audience will tolerate jargon and dull writing. In fact, they may expect you to use convoluted writing conventions and diction as a kind of cultural sign of your seriousness and intelligence. If you write like a novelist, an academic audience might even be suspicious that you are making stuff up.

You can write well no matter what your audience, but different people in different situations have different standards for what constitutes good writing. Not only do you need to consider the contexuality and intercontextuality of your fieldwork. You need to consider writing as a contextual and intercontextual act.

In all these cases, you must choose between short-form and long-form styles. For an academic audience, will you be writing a journal article or an academic book?

Journals themselves come in various flavors, and choosing the proper one dictates the kind of work that you must do. A generalist disciplinary journal will speak to everyone in your discipline. This means that your work needs to speak to a problem that is of wide import to the field. It also means that you will likely need to explain your theoretical concepts in more depth, since not all readers will have read the literature that you're citing. The generalist disciplinary journals can be the hardest to publish in and are best suited to publishing the largest and strongest themes in your work.

An interdisciplinary journal that connects to your research area can also be a good choice. Interdisciplinary journals will want your work to speak to wide issues as well, but often without the theoretical focus of a disciplinary journal. Instead, an interdisciplinary journal is often looking for the usefulness of your work: Does it have implications for policy or methodology? Scholars in other disciplines can use this information to inform their own work, even if they might disagree with the theoretical underpinnings.

A specialist journal will let you go in depth, sacrificing the number of readers in favor of discussion with other specialists on your topic. While you might be tempted to think that this is where the most prestigious journals are—since the vetting can be strongest when the reviewers are also specialists in your topic—specialist journals are among the least prestigious areas to publish in, for two reasons. First, your work will not be read by as many readers. Second, the act of translating your work for more general audiences usually makes your work stronger. While specialists can critique your work from within a perspective, your work will usually be most improved by answering the questions that are raised from outsiders, thus becoming more multilogical.

We suggest for that reason that, if you are pursuing a journal article, you first attempt to publish for a general audience. If your work is not then chosen for publication, at least the review process will have made it stronger and more useful to outsiders. That way, even if it is published in a specialist journal, it still has the likelihood of being used by others.

Starting to see how writing decisions influence contestability and narrativity? Your choice of venue influences who is going to be reading your work. Someone from an interdisciplinary journal has different expectations of evidence to someone in your flagship journal. It isn't just that you are presenting your work differently; your project is a different project when considered from another perspective.

Surprisingly, considering the length and stress of the review process, journal articles can be one of the quickest ways to disseminate academic work—mostly because writing a journal article can be a fairly quick affair. As Belcher says, in her book *Writing Your Journal Article in 12 Weeks*, the standard format of the journal article makes it relatively simple to mimic.[1] Look at articles in the journal you wish to publish in and you'll see that most follow a standard pattern and length. The methods section might discuss issues like sampling and field site for 500 words, while ignoring methods of analysis, such as how you coded. The conclusion might address policy implications for 300 words and suggestions for future research for another 200. Using these as models, writing your article becomes a matter of filling in the blanks with your research.

Academic books are the long-form style of the academic audience. A book will have looser requirements for organization than a journal article, which means that the difficulty of writing it increases, not only because of length but also because of the variety of organizational structures for presenting your case you will need to consider. An academic book also must consider different audiences: Who will be reading this book? Often, this question turns into another one: What level of scholars will be reading my book? Undergraduates or graduate students and professors?

A book written for graduate students and professors will oscillate between a depth suited to a generalist journal article and the treatment of material suited to a specialist journal. But a book is not just a patchwork of journal articles. You will need to consider the ***meta-narrative***—the implicit narrative—and the structure of the book as a whole. We discuss these issues later in the chapter.

Some among you—undergraduate and graduate students, perhaps reading this book for a class—will wonder: "What if I don't care about either of these venues? I just want to write my thesis and graduate!" It's true. A research paper, a thesis, and a dissertation are different beasts from a journal article or a book. The contexts and intercontexts of their situations differ markedly. However, your advisor, professor, or committee are merely stand-ins for these wider audiences. If you are collecting data—and you're reading this book, so you are—then your work shouldn't be limited to your committee.

Ideally, this would mean that you would actually write as though you were submitting to one of these venues from the beginning. Jason wrote his master's thesis as a journal article and his dissertation as a book. His committee had suggestions and demands regarding both, but having a future venue with a clear organization structure helped him define his saturation point and clarified his arguments.

Your committee might not be willing to share its power with the dictates of outside readers, however. If that's the case, follow their wishes, but keep your eventual publication in mind. It will be more work, but you should always attempt to get your research published for all of the work you have already put into it. Frankly, the They—your participants and communities—deserve no less for the time and effort you demanded of them. Nonetheless, many students are burned out by the time they finish their thesis or dissertation, or get caught up in the demands of a job or their home life. Even when it is well done, much—maybe most—student research never emerges from the shelves of libraries where they were deposited. By virtue of working in the area, collecting data, conversing with scholars and participants, and working through your own positionality, you developed unique perspectives. So stick it out! You are an important part of the public conversation of research.

However, as Hagger-Johnson and colleagues argue, we should avoid a "deficit model" in which we assume that the public does not know what we are talking about.[2] Strive for a "bidirectional knowledge transfer," as the psychologists put it, seeking to publish as much to learn from others as to share your findings. Consider balancing your academic writing with publishing in popular venues.

Not all writing must be done with a public audience in mind. Journal articles and academic books are useful for researchers. Conversation with other academics encourages the clarification of concepts and opens up new boundaries for research. Writing for non-academic audiences, though, lets your data gathering continue even after your fieldwork ends, when you hear feedback from the public—even if it's negative!

Plus, popular writing allows you to address parts of your research that academic journals and books might not allow you to foreground. For instance, what are the policy implications of your ethnography? What does your work say about how people should manage their lives and relationships? An often untold part of our work is an ethical dimension: what should people do, not just what they are doing. Writing for non-academics lets you consider the ethical or normative dimension of your work, and invite public conversation about it.

Sometimes all this can be done in a single publication—addressing both popular and academic audiences—much as Mike attempted in his book *Farming for Us All*. By writing the book as though farmers and eaters were going to read it, he got a chance to explain some of the implications of his work that might actually help change the socially and ecologically damaging way we grow our food. But it's a hard balance to maintain. Mike's not sure he always managed it. The risk is that you miss both audiences at once.

The solution? Try to get even more logics into your book by inviting readers from a wide range of backgrounds to read your work before you publish it. And ideally while you are still writing it, so you are in a better position to change course, if need be. Send early chapters of your work to friends and relatives. And form a writing group with colleagues, sharing critiques of each other's emerging works. You have to be prepared for others not necessarily liking your stuff and even getting a bit riled up about it. Their reactions may not always be gently put. But don't lose heart. Better to hear all that now, before you publish, and consider whether they are right or whether their negative reactions actually suggest that your work usefully touches a social sore spot.

And it is lovely and empowering when they say nice things!

Most often though, due to factors like funding, the job market, or tenure decisions, we might have to publish more exclusively academic work and keep non-academic work separate.

Social Science Art

But here's another, and increasingly reputable, approach: *Social science art*—using the sensibilities and forms of art within academic social scientific work. Social science art can be a powerful way to present data and theory in a way that circumvents the standard rational response. Instead, social science art evokes an emotional response that draws on intuitive knowledge of the ideas you are attempting to convey.

One example of social science art is *research poetry*. Consider the short poem, "White I" from the book *Water in a Dry Land* by Margaret Somerville:

> **White I**
>
> White is
> not a colour
> I usually write.[3]

Short, very short to be sure. But Somerville uses this pithy poem to orient the reader to the emotional task of a white writer writing the story of Aboriginal lands and peoples.

Poetry is not the only form of art that can communicate to readers. Poetry can sometimes be alienating, especially to those without a humanities or liberal arts background. Somerville also uses painting and images to communicate to readers—often maps produced by Aboriginal people themselves. Photography can directly confront readers with the image of your participants and their environments. The work of the visual ethnographer Douglas Harper is a case in point. As Harper notes, "images allow us to make statements which cannot be made by words," and thereby "enlarge our consciousness and the possibilities" for our scholarship.[4] Images appeal to the fullness of the reader as a person, for we are all more than merely rational. And not just photographs: images of all kinds. (That's why we include the images by Matt Raboin, an artist friend of ours, at the chapter openings of this book.)

In *The Strange Music of Social Life: A Dialogue on Dialogic Sociology*, Mike uses yet another approach.[5] He happens to be a part-time composer, so he wrote a piece that embodied an argument he wanted to make—not surprisingly, an argument about the multilogical character of social life! A classical group performed and recorded the piece. Mike then sent the recording to 10 academics, along with a paper about what he was trying to achieve with the music and the performance. (Mike's academic point had to do with the potential creativity of social interaction, when different logics come together.) The 10 academics wrote papers in response, and Mike wrote a response to their responses. And that's the book—a multilogical dialogue about multilogical dialogue, as experienced through music.

Another use of social science art is as an alternative form of expression for participants. What Harper says about images allowing us to make statements that are hard to put into words also applies to our research participants. Researchers often ask hard questions that require people to articulate what they generally don't think about linguistically. So consider using art with your participants in your next project. A community group could work together on a video about their neighborhood, revealing their lens on issues there. The Belgian agroecologist Pierre Stassart and his colleagues tried this— they called it "participatory film-making"—with a group of part-time livestock farmers. What scenes the farmers chose to include and not to include and the discussions they had over their joint film-making project gave Stassart and his colleagues rich and surprising data about the meaning the farmers found in their work.[6] They found that art can be yet another interpretive tool to help us break past the standard response set of what people already know how to articulate.

But even if you don't think of it this way, all academic writing and all the evidence you gather from your participants has elements of art in it. It's all communication. The Russian composer Modest Mussorgsky used to say that all art is a form of communication.[7] To which we would add, all communication is a form of art. Even when you are writing as dully as you can, because you think the venue for your writing requires you to, you are still using your creative skills to appear as unexciting as possible! So why not be conscious of what you are trying to do?

Narrativity and Partiality

What are we supposed to take from all of this discussion of venues and audiences? How does it help us produce writing that will be truthful and useful to all three logics in a situation: They, You, and We?

We believe the answer lies in acknowledging the partiality that is inherent in writing and considering some of the narrative choices one must make in dealing with that partiality. Part of the story will always be told elsewhere—and sometimes nowhere at all. We will probably never have the kind of access to the They voice that You had. The We has to rely on You as a conduit to They.

Acknowledging that partiality—that We will never hear your participants completely—can be immobilizing. It can turn someone off the whole qualitative enterprise. How can something so partial even be science?

But once we realize that all science is partial, we can work together to fill in the blanks. If we think of truth not as flat but as a many-sided jewel, glittering with light from many directions and perspectives, then we can expect any one fieldwork project to cut and reflect only one, two, or at most a few of its facets. To construct the whole, we have to talk with each other to find out their perspectives, their experiences, their logics. And there is much to celebrate in this partiality. It gives all of us the opportunity to tell our perspectives in dialogue with each other. Diverse venues and audiences also give us multiple opportunities to emphasize different facets.

Partiality also means that a significant responsibility comes with writing. The person that writes a piece exerts considerable control over the story. Even if people within your community, your participants, manage to respond later to your work, you will have already set the terms of the debate. People often talk about how the winners of a war control history because they write the story of what happened. No matter the method, all social science shares in that burden—even participatory research.

You have to be fair to what and who are being reported. Who is speaking? Who is being implicitly represented by the individuals in your work, especially those from organizations with their own agendas?

In some ways, journalists have a head start on field researchers in the social sciences in acknowledging their responsibilities in these areas, because often the people they are talking to are not anonymous. It is also customary in their profession to ask for comments from opposing parties before they publish something negative. The presumption is that they are going to call other people to comment on the story that they are reporting, to make sure that others have the chance to speak for themselves.

We can mimic this in our science through the principles of disconfirming information and member checking that we've discussed previously. While these are good tools for the gathering of data and the design of the project, they are also narrative strategies to address the partiality of your work and make it contestable.

For disconfirming information, make sure that the text answers the questions that your readers will likely have about your work and acknowledge aspects of your work that do not, or did not initially, fit within your theory. By demonstrating to the audience that you challenged yourself, it will be evident that you are incorporating a variety of perspectives, a variety of facets, which in turn inform your own.

For member checking, include in the text moments when participants may be seen to be talking to one another about similar issues, even though they didn't know each other or were not in the same situation. Particularly useful are any moments where participants might have disagreed with you. These quotes indicate that you appreciate the messy world behind your data and did not clean it up to make it fit nicely into a book or article. This kind of *heteroglossia* demonstrates that while you have narrative control, the They voice of your project is present in the piece.

Disagreement, however, doesn't mean that you are wrong in your assessment of the issues. You've done your due diligence in contending with the multiplicity and singularity of the problem you are studying. Your participants quite likely have not. Just because they disagree with you, or someone in the audience disagrees with you, or even a reviewer or committee member or professor disagrees with you, does not mean that they are right. While you must contend with the responsibility of narrative control, you still need to control the narrative so your perspective—and by extension, the They voice of your participants—can still come through. That is another important responsibility.

Therefore, don't be afraid to make the case that you are an authority, an expert in your project and issue. You studied, perhaps for years, to become an expert. You may feel a bit guilty about this. You may feel like you are making a bit of a grab for power. And you are. But that power is not only your own if you are responsive to your professional training, to the social significance of your work, and to the words and actions of your participants. And if your work is to be valuable, it has to be valued—to be recognized as trustworthy and authoritative from the perspective of the social scientific fieldworker.

In traditional and positivist science, scholars often seek implicit authority by obscuring the decisions made in the research. By filling the text with jargon and not explaining underlying methodology, the positive scientist relies on authority by virtue of status: I have a PhD, so trust me.

That probably won't work for you. The multilogical scientist establishes authority through transparency. Reporting your methods accurately, as we discuss in the next section, allows readers to judge for themselves whether you know what you are doing—whether you took reasonable steps to ensure the quality of your analysis. As well, it gives readers the opportunity to add their own knowledge and experiences to those that you present in the text, bringing yet more logics to bear on the work.

It is also important to write about your mistakes. Both Jason and Mike do this in their work. Among other things, it helps readers understand the thought process behind your analysis. Seeing where you went wrong helps readers see where you went right. In addition, it humanizes the text. No one is perfect. There will be times in an interview when you lead the participant with a question. There will be times when the community group that you are working with makes a decision that is wrong for the project. It is going to happen.

For the most part, your readers also know that it is going to happen. If you attempt to cover these mistakes up, then it actually discredits your work. When Jason is reviewing a manuscript, for instance, one of the marks of quality he looks for is first an acknowledgement of error and then what the author attempted to do to fix it. By establishing that you are someone who is transparent about your mistakes and that you take active steps to prevent an error from happening again, you show your audience that your work is contestable. They are not going to assume that there are grave errors lurking just off the page just because you admitted to some right on the page. If anything, the reverse is likely. Because you encourage the reader to read multilogically if you write multilogically.

All these techniques of mulitlogical writing—presenting disconfirming evidence, member checking, transparent methods, and presenting errors—need to be presented in the text no matter what venue you choose. To get there, though, it takes more than the hard work that you put in to collect the data. You have to actually write.

Writing Multilogically

We've considered some of the theory behind multilogical writing, but not any of the practicalities of writing. What does a multilogical methods section look like? How do multilogically informed researchers create literature reviews? Perhaps most importantly, how do you actually get any writing done? As the two writers of this book, we take different roads to arrive at similar answers to these questions. Jason works top-down from an extensive outline. Mike starts at the beginning of a text with only a very general outline of what is to come, allowing the logic of argument to develop as the writing proceeds. J. K. Rowling works like Jason. Mike writes more like Stephen King. Although writers might work differently, there are some commonalities to writing multilogically.

For instance, although the method we use to create is different, both of us agree that a strong organizational structure reinforces the narrative thread of your work. The basic organization of your text is dictated by the venue you are publishing in and its audience. Journals have one way of doing things. Books have another.

Yet, that is often where many authors stop considering their organization, merely copying the section titles from what they model their work on, without considering the purpose of the organization. The structure of a paper or chapter helps guide your readers through your argument. An introduction doesn't only get people excited about the rest of the text, it should tell them where they can find the answers to their questions about your project. A literature review can actually hinder understanding if it merely dumps a bunch of citations without building knowledge. Let's walk through each of the sections and consider the tools for success.

The Lead

As we just mentioned, an introduction should catch the reader's attention, excite them about the chapter, and provide a guide to where in the manuscript they can find information. A good opening or "lead" will accomplish all of these goals.

A common form of lead in fieldwork is an "entry trope"—a description of what it is like to approach the field site from afar, or an account of an individual (usually the author) who is entering the site or who is immersed in it, so as to draw the reader in. A particularly famous entry trope launches Clifford Geertz's widely reprinted ethnographic essay, "Notes on the Balinese Cockfight," in which Geertz and his wife are chased through a Balinese village by the police, who have come to break up a cockfight they were watching.[8] Mike's *Childerley* takes gentler approach, describing a "narrow, single-lane road [which] emerges from the dark, sunken passage through the bluebell wood" and leads to "Childerley," painting "an introduction to the village as the villagers like to think of it."[9] Although neither author makes it explicit, the entry trope leads the reader into the setting and asks for their suspension of disbelief and hostility, as the reader identifies with Geertz and his wife or with Childerley's villagers' vision of their home. An entry trope is an example of a *meta-narrative*, a story behind the story, which the author does not state outright but that is built into the structure of the narrative.

Your lead is also crucial for establishing ***narrative permission***—the reader's tolerance for the kind of writing you want to do. We judge different kinds of writing from the vantage point of very different expectations. An article in a top professional journal probably couldn't get away with a beginning like the one J. K. Rowling used to open the first *Harry Potter* novel:

> Mr. and Mrs. Dursley, of number four, Privet Drive, were proud to say that they were perfectly normal, thank you very much. They were the last people you'd expect to be involved in anything strange or mysterious, because they just didn't hold with such nonsense.[10]

Expect instead the statement of a scientific issue, some professional jargon, and several references to scientific literature. Take for example the opening of the lead article in the April, 2013 issue of the *American Sociological Review*:

> Race is associated with profound levels of social and economic stratification that pre-date the founding of our country and survive robustly to this day. Even with the recent re-election of our first African American president in what some call a post-racial society, residential segregation remains extreme, and racial inequalities in educational and occupational attainment, income, home ownership, quality of life, health, and mortality remain stark (Farley and Frey 1994; Feagin 2001; Massey and Denton 1998; Oliver and Shapiro 2006; Sorlie, Backlund, and Keller 1995; Thomas and Hughes 1998; Williams and Collins 1995).[11]

One only has to read a few lines (and perhaps even just the first few words) to know what kind of piece each is and what kind of standards the work seeks to be evaluated by (if we may callously dangle a participle here). The *ASR* piece asks the reader's permission to write something that is technical and a bit difficult to read. J. K. Rowling asks to be allowed to write something that doesn't tax the reader's technical capacities and is difficult to put down. But this permission fast becomes a command. Once you ask permission to be evaluated in some way, you'd better be able to meet those standards.

The activeness of your voice strongly shapes the reader's sense of narrative permission. Look again at the J. K. Rowling example. She puts active agents right at the very beginning of her entire work, "Mr. and Mrs. Dursley, of number four, Privet Drive," who "were proud to say that they were perfectly normal, thank you very much." We will now expect entertainingly active writing for the rest of work—a promise that J. K. Rowling keeps famously well.

The *ASR* piece, on the other hand, slides agency under the dark waters of passive construction, right from its opening phrase: "Race is associated with profound levels of social and economic stratification … ." Really? Who makes this association? The article does not say, although it implies the association maker is the all-knowing, all-pervasive, God-like eye of science. The article legitimates this implication at the end of the second sentence, with a barrage of seven citations (including some major names in that area of research). OK, so now we know. This work of writing does not claim to entertain. It holds our attention through its ability to keep to a dispassionate narrative of truth so impartial that it has no agents, with all their corrupting feelings and politics. But imagine if it had begun this way: "The all-knowing, all-pervasive, God-like eye of science associates race with profound levels of social and economic stratification," poking fun at the very idea of agent-less research. The reviewers (perhaps the most important audience for any scholarly work) would have immediately pounded REJECT into their emails back to the editor.

If this sounds like we're writing a screenplay and not a journal article, don't worry. Mike and Jason both use ethnographic scenes from their work as their usual leads, sounding more like J. K. Rowling or Stephen King than that *ASR* article, and they still manage to get published in academic venues! Other authors use participants' quotes, popular culture discussion, or puzzles within the academic literature, attempting to invoke various metanarrative forms of identification from the reader. However you begin, you really can't avoid having a "lead." You have to start somewhere, and your choice matters a lot for what readers will allow you to do afterwards.

Constructing leads is fairly simple because they follow similar narrative arcs. Leads for write-ups of fieldwork usually seek permission to describe real lives and to use some of the forms of writing one might find in J. K. Rowling, while still hoping to hold on to the readers of a venue like the *American Sociological Review*. So fieldwork leads typically start in the middle of an action: interviewing a participant, entering a scene, describing an incident. This creates a sense of urgency within the text that you will build up in subsequent paragraphs.

In long-form writing, you might be able to keep your lead going for several pages, but in typical articles your lead should be short, in the order of a few paragraphs, if not just one. Describe the action, without getting overly lost in describing every aspect of the scene. Your lead's action should end with a question to which your argument proposes the answer. This acts as a kind of narrative cliff. Your audience is stopped short after running forward with the action. Suddenly, they catch themselves at the edge, over which they can see the whole of the rest of your chapter or paper. In that moment, you end your lead with a guide to the rest of your paper's sections and proceed to the next part.

The Literature Review

In many venues, the next section catches the reader up with key concepts they will need to understand your argument. In academic parlance, we call this the literature review—probably the part of an academic paper that authors most hate to write and readers most hate to read.

Those new to writing literature reviews will often be given the following advice: Review two or more areas of knowledge and point out a gap between them, the thing they missed. That gap is your argument.

This is wrong. Do not do this.

Such a vision of scholarship puts your work in an adversarial relationship with earlier work. Idiots! See what they missed? How could they have? They must have been blinded by bad method and bad theory. Fortunately, I am here to rescue science from the errors of these deviants.

Go this way and you produce a divisive meta-narrative: Someone else has to have done something wrong for you to be doing something right. There, now you've gone and annoyed everyone on both sides of your gap. And in a few years, someone else will be saying the same nasty things about you.

Instead, we prefer the metaphor of *bridge building*, bringing literatures together rather than creating gaps. Use your literature review to stimulate the conversation by bringing different logics together. Guide readers towards knowledge in areas of academia they have not explored yet. Be a uniter, not a divider.

In this way, you'll also have dealt with one of the great terrors of the academic: that you've been scooped. So many academics seem to sneak around hoping that no one is going fling at them that reference they should have read and that seems to say exactly what *they* say at some point in their write-up. Poof! There goes your claim to originality. Your gap has already been filled. So you wind up hating and fearing the academic literature. Given that you are trying to contribute to that literature, it's a woeful paradox. It doesn't feel good.

But if you are a bridge-builder, it is wonderful to hear about other literature. See? Someone else supports my point here! Another voice speaks with me. Someone else will be interested in what I find out. Now you are no longer scared to "review" the literature.

Now, you may still worry: What if someone else makes the exact same argument as me, throughout—not merely saying what I say at a few points in my case?

Come on. How likely is that? You are you. And the They you studied are who they are. The two are almost certain to have come together differently with different results to what might have been the case with different researchers at a different time and place. The partiality and difference of your research now becomes not the death-knell of a consistent science but the source of science's originality.

If you follow the gap-filling model, so often counseled as the way to make an original contribution, you are likely to be original only in the most dispiriting of ways: by making a ever-narrower point about the shrinking space between ever-growing literatures. Yes, original, but so knit-picky that you can barely describe its value to anyone not intimately familiar with the scholarship you are arguing against, hoping to hold those sides from squishing you entirely into oblivion.

But if you take a bridge-building approach, you don't even need to worry about being original. You're a conversation-starter. And the conversation can be as big as you want it to be. Make it big enough, build enough bridges, and there are sure to be new connections to make. Indeed, that's exactly what both bridge-building and originality are: new connections.

In this way the dreaded literature review becomes a positive experience that leaves you feeling good about your contribution, about other scholars, and even about yourself.

Besides, you probably shouldn't even think about this section as "reviewing" the literature —an impossible task, anyway, given how much has already been written about everything. Think about it this way instead: What you are doing is introducing two (or more) communities of scholarship to each other. Making academic friends. Of course, there are still more communities to bring into the conversation. But you've made a start, and the reader can clearly appreciate that you've done enough. So the bridge-building model also has the additional advantage of preventing your literature from spiraling out of control and turning into a beast that rapidly takes over your whole article, and still doesn't seem like enough. Bridge-building connects but also bounds.

Plus, the literature review section motivates readers to see your data. After all of this preparation—a climactic lead that gave them a taste and a review that piqued their interest in your argument—they want to see what you've done.

In a long-form academic piece or a piece for public consumption, let them have it. Start laying out the evidence supporting your argument. But in a journal article, your reader has one more question before they are ready to see your data: What did you do? Why should I believe you?

Methods and Results

Your methods section answers these questions for the reader by accurately describing how you gathered your evidence. This section can be tricky, though, because you must balance the proper amount of detail. Say too little and the audience will not be convinced that you used appropriate methods to arrive at your conclusion. Give them too much and they are going to wonder why you are so defensive about your work.

For these reasons, when writing a methods section for a journal, we like to keep it short by touching on three areas. We identify the overall mix of approaches that we took: interviews, ethnographic, participatory. We give information about the depth and breadth of our sample: Who did we talk to and how long were we there? Finally, we briefly explain our strategy of analysis. We leave out long discussions of methodology (the theory of methods), defenses of low-*n* research, and explanations of common qualitative strategies because these will make your work unnecessarily defensive. Assume that the professional reader will appreciate qualitative methods because they are accepted practices and it is more likely that they will be. We get back from this digression into methods as quickly as possible so we can discuss what readers really want to know: your results.

Bear this in mind when you get to your results section. (This may be one of the few jabs in this book at the qualitative vs. quantitative divide, but it does not seem controversial.) Qualitative work is often more enjoyable to read. It usually feels more like J. K. Rowling than that article we quote from the *American Journal of Sociology.* Qualitative work connects us to other people by hearing about their lives and speaking in their voices. So, don't drown those voices out when writing "results" or using your data to convey your argument.

Too often, qualitative writers create a "patchwork quilt" of quotes. Perhaps due to insecurity about the evidence they are providing, they will overwhelm the reader with quotes or scenes, drowning them in evidence. And perhaps out of an implicitly quantitative mentality, some qualitative writers seem to feel that every point needs to be documented with many instances. But an appreciation of singularity should teach us not to confuse significance with abundance. Many of the most important clues you get in your research will occur only once. Indeed, if we take singularity seriously, nothing ever exactly repeats.

Ultimately, a patchwork quilt approach to data undermines your position for two reasons. First, it implies that there is something to be hidden. Writers provide overwhelming evidence to counter the common argument that they are cherry-picking quotes. Yet, when they provide too many, readers will question what they left out. Were these the only quotes they had on the subject? If there are five quotes in the text about an issue, why is it not six?

Second, the patchwork quilt encourages decontextualization. Put in all those short quotes, and you won't have enough space to analyze the nuances of any quote or scene. All venues have space requirements. By the time that you've finished describing in detail the three different times that you saw this phenomenon out in the field, there will not be space to explain the meaning behind these scenes. You've lost the multiplicity involved in any real context.

Research is not only about description. We must also use our knowledge as researchers to extrapolate from these scenes—to reach from contextuality into intercontextuality. The patchwork quilt skips us from scene to scene, quote to quote, without allowing the reader time to absorb their import, or for you to bring out specificities that yield generalities.

The solution to these issues is to develop an argument and present evidence only towards that argument. You'll need to carry your argument right through your evidence. Don't just put the argument in the beginning of the paper and assume the reader will sift through your favorite quotes and incidents and follow why you included these quotes and incidents—especially if really haven't thought that through yourself. Remind the reader along the way what significance you are taking from the evidence. Divide your argument thematically or along a causal path or chain, showing evidence for each of the viewpoints or steps along that path and how the evidence fits with your theoretical categories.

By doing it this way, you've ensured that the reader has evidence for each of your claims and that you are only using quotes or scenes as representations of a particular viewpoint and as steps toward understanding its context. Your work no longer becomes an amalgam of every single data point you have. Deploying data in this way also forces you to make sure that your argument moves beyond the descriptive, since you will have to support each section with adequate theorizing and analysis.

It also means—perhaps painfully—that you show only a small proportion of your evidence. So much good stuff that you don't use! But it's all actually still there, shaping how you interpret everything you do include.

So are you being selective, then? Yes. For sure. You are choosing the evidence that is most illustrative, given the small amount of space you have. And you are reporting it with lots of the multiplicity of context, giving the reader the ability to make another interpretation, in case you got something wrong. You are actually hiding less than if you try to overwhelm the reader with tons of bits of de-contextualized stuff that they can't challenge because you haven't told them enough about any one bit.

We recommend several tools to support a more multilogical approach to writing results. First, try presenting your data as vignettes. A vignette is a small scene that departs from the style and tone of the main text, a step into another writing zone and space. Vignettes allow you to discuss in detail a scene or quote. Not all your data should necessarily be presented in vignettes, however. They are particularly useful at the beginning of a section or introduction because they let you thoroughly describe an issue that you can then elaborate on in your main text.

Vignettes are also a way of deploying a second tool: Geertz's notion of "thick description" that we discussed in the chapter on Looking. Using thick description means recreating a scene in such detail that the audience will be able to imagine themselves there without having to experience the moment. Neither of us have been to a cockfight, or been chased by police afterwards, but Geertz's famous description has given us a visceral and lasting image.

The danger of thick description is that it is easy to include irrelevant details that distract readers from your argument. Every aspect of your paper or chapter should be providing evidence that builds towards your conclusion. Limit extraneous details to those that reveal an aspect of your participant's character, the context, or your methodological procedures.

Another tool that helps prevent the patchwork quilt is presenting another style of data alongside the main text—visual ethnography, for example. Venues may resist adding these kinds of elements, if you suggest them after the fact. In an interesting twist, though, providing them upon submission of your paper, book, or article will make them much more likely to be accepted, because the editors will be more likely to feel a connection to your work. A word of warning, however: Make sure you consider the ethical quandaries of visual presentation before making the leap, especially issues of confidentiality.

Finally, the tone of the piece—the way in which you present the data in a particular voice—should reinforce your method. On the two extremes, you have positivistic and novelistic styles of voicing. A positivistic style is the traditional academic voice: jargon-filled, obscure, and hiding the agent and analyzer of the work. However, in its favor, it is no-nonsense in organization and helps keep the reader firmly aware of how your evidence connects to your argument.

The novelistic style, that we tend to use, focuses on using plain language and writing data as though it was a story. Novelistic voicing strays too far, though, when it obscures the argument in favor of narrative tension. Although the line between the two is less firm than it perhaps seemed to Mike's questioner at his job talk, fiction and social science are different narrative forms, with different standards of evaluation. Establishing an argument remains key to the social science narrative. Your reader should know up-front the point you are trying to make, even as you endeavor to give some life to the participants in your text. In this way, you can take the best of both styles of voicing.

Getting It Out the Door

How do we get all of this writing done? By reading a lot, talking a lot, and—most importantly—writing a lot. Good writers are good readers. They sample other authors' styles and voices. They think not only about the meaning of an author's text but also how the author conveyed that meaning. They consider how they can best contribute to the conversation of culture and scholarship.

Talking to others about your work is also immensely helpful. To explain something to someone else is also to explain it to yourself. Present to your colleagues and at conferences. Talk to your partner about what you're finding. Play the "bus stop game" with colleagues, where you pretend to explain the gist of your work to a perfect stranger in about a minute. Heck, play the bus stop game on a bus with real strangers! And listen to how your logic, based on the logics you encountered in the field, intersects with the logics of those who might very well be in the audience of your writing one day.

It might also help to take a step back into your field site or talk to participants again if you feel that you're having trouble writing. These interactions can energize you, reminding you of aspects of your work that you might have forgotten in the zeal to get every comma placed correctly, as well as reminding you of the passion that brought you to the work to begin with. Participants can also point out crucial things that they never thought worth noting before, or that you never thought worth taking note of. Huge breakthroughs often happen in this way.

And, as we said, write a lot. We don't necessarily mean write your book or article. Write lots of things—and not just emails and text messages! Write memos. Keep a journal. Pen a poem. Make charts and Venn diagrams. Show it to others, both to get their feedback, their logics, and also to get used to showing your work to others.

You may feel under pressure, and worry that writing anything that isn't the actual book or article is a waste of time. And then the fingers freeze and the words don't come, making matters only worse. So keep the words flowing, always flowing, so that fear doesn't settle on your keys.

The way that you start writing can help you actually write, instead of staring at the blank white screen each day. Jason uses a journal—an idea he took from Julia Cameron's "Morning Pages"—to pre-write before starting a day's writing. The stream of consciousness style that it provokes warms up his fingers, and reminds him that the words don't have to be perfect before they go down on the page. It helps jump-start his process.

Similarly, Mike gets in the zone by revising the previous day's work. Reading it over, he can make small edits and start to grab the thread he left dangling at the end of the last session. By the time he gets to the blank area, he's already found the words for what needs to be expressed next.

This might be one reason why many famous writers recommend leaving your writing each day with an unfinished sentence. Or stopping just before you find yourself out of steam. By ending on a high note, with the last thought left unexpressed, it can be a bit easier to slip back into that state of flow, carrying you ever forward toward fulfilling the promise of fieldwork.

Recipes for Writing

1. Voicing

The Passive voice is the writing of science.

Scientists write using the passive voice.

There are many different ways that one can voice the same sentiment. Academics often choose the voice that will obscure their role in the production of the work and make a work more difficult for everyone to understand.

In this exercise, write about a situation in two different styles. First, take data from a collection exercise in previous chapters or from your own work. Write about that observation, scene, or quote using a positivistic passive science voice, as often found in academic journals. Then, write that scene again in a novelistic style that foregrounds your voice and role in the production of this piece of knowledge.

2. Academic Art

This exercise is always met with the a lot of skepticism every time we have taught it in a methods class. We love it anyway.

Choose a style of artistic representation: poetry, creative nonfiction, fiction, music, painting, sculpture, dance, etc.

Create a piece in this style that evokes the arguments, topics, and problems present in your project.

For an in-depth example, see Mike's book *Strange Music* (Bell 2011), in which he composed a musical piece to evoke the concept of "strangency" as opposed to control.

3. Fiction for Nonfiction's Sake

On the surface, this exercise might seem to be the same as the last. After all, you will also be creating a piece of art. However, the goal is different.

For this exercise, write a short story set within your field site or featuring problems faced by your participants.

The goal is not to create a work that represents. Instead, this is practice for you to release your inner positivist critic and try novelistic-style writing. After writing a piece of fiction, using the same voice in a work of nonfiction will seem easier and more natural.

For this reason, don't neglect reading fiction (and poetry if you enjoy it). Jason tries to read at least one book of fiction a semester to keep in the habit of enjoying new words, organizations, and sentence structures. (Plus, it's fun!)

4. Venues

Unabashedly, we think that you should publish in more kinds of venues. Not just journals, not just books, but news panels, magazine articles, presentations, and art.

Use the chart below (Table 8.1) to help brainstorm venues where your work could be presented in different ways.

Here are a few:

A: Your disciplinary organization almost certainly has a newsletter. Is there anything about your project you would want other academics to know that would be inappropriate for a scientific article or academic book?

B: Academics sit in silos too much, largely presenting only to conferences in their own speciality. Do some digging and go to a conference which is focused on your topic area or in a discipline not your own.

C: The groups you work with, even if they weren't participants that you conducted member checking with, deserve to know about your work. Write a short op-ed, magazine article, or even blog post that would be enjoyed by your participants.

D. Step out of your comfort zone. Go to an open-mic night and present some academic art.

Table 8.1

		Short	Presentations	Media	Art
Disciplinary				A	
Interdisciplinary			B		
Your Participants/field		C			
The General Public					D

5. Results by Numbers

Like painting by numbers, a quick way to organize a results section or a chapter's argument is by finding quotes or scenes and letting them guide you during your writing. By identifying a single scene or quote for each part of your argument, this organizational strategy can help prevent both the patchwork quilt of quotes and overwhelming presentations of evidence.

Your argument requires evidence for readers to believe it. On the front of a set of notecards, break down your argument into smaller claims that support it. If you're having trouble, on the back of each card identify one scene or participant quote for each claim.

Arranging these in order is a rudimentary outline that you can use to quickly write your piece.

People are complex
And they are creative,
juggling the demands and
they face, searching for new
Sometimes they find them, and the
theory that made sense in a previous
no longer seems so apt. The field
close enough to the spark and
real social life that very often
he can see the change
or at least its first
flames.
With fieldwork, you get a chance to
at the Metropolitan
technique at the
and talking
there are no final
being given a
an openness to the wonder of the
which, after
Perhaps, the
no final

9
The Promise of Fieldwork

A few years ago, Mike's children's "English grandmother" died. It was sad, of course. Kath was a wonderful woman who sat at the center of a vast network of family and friends. But it was a moment for celebration too—celebration of 84 years well lived. For Mike, it was also a moment for celebrating the fulfillment of the promise of fieldwork. Because Kath was not a blood relative. She was someone Mike had met 25 years earlier while doing the ethnographic fieldwork for *Childerley*, his study of nature and social class in exurban England that we've already mentioned a few times in this book. Kath was a key participant in the story. Mike quoted her often in *Childerley* (using a pseudonym). But she was much more than that. She and her husband Doug became close friends, almost family. Mike and his wife brought their children to visit them several times in England, and one summer Kath and Doug's own children scraped up the funds—the family is working class, so this was quite an undertaking—to buy them first class tickets to fly to the US to spend a couple of weeks vacationing with Mike's family. (It was the first time either had been on a plane.) Kath even knitted sweaters for both her "American grandchildren," as she called Mike's kids. The families continued to exchange letters, cards, and phone calls right up until Kath's death.

This doesn't happen with survey research.

Which is immediately one good answer to the question we take up in this, the final chapter: Why do fieldwork anyway? Or, to restate the question in the terms we've been developing in the book, what promise does fieldwork hold for the They, for the You, and for the We voices of research? Because there are plenty of reasons to try some other approach. Fieldwork can take a long time. It's often confusing and frustrating. Many find it lonely, especially at the beginning of a project. You spend a lot of time worrying about the social relations of your fieldwork, when you've already got plenty of troubles in your personal life (if you're like most folks). Plus, although the scientific status of fieldwork methods has risen markedly in recent years, many scholars still don't give it a lot of respect and it still doesn't often make it into the top academic journals.

So let's consider the promise of fieldwork, beginning first with what it holds for the We, then the You, and finally the They.

The Promise for the We

Methodologists often like to assess the ***reliability*** and the ***validity*** of a method. It's a classic distinction. Reliable methods give the same answer time and again, across differences in sample and in the researchers themselves. Jason, Mike, you: If we all get the same or similar results from the same method with similar populations, we can consider that method reliable. Survey methods are famous for their reliability. Everything is tightly controlled and repeatable. Not so qualitative fieldwork. Even if you, Mike, and Jason all went out to interview the same people about the same topics, we are virtually certain to come back with differing results. Why? Because we are all different, and the same people will respond differently to each of us. The inherent interactiveness of fieldwork means the researchers' differences will be part of the data, as we discussed earlier in the book.

For many, this variability damns fieldwork to the purgatory of scientific fiction. But survey methods have their own epistemological sticky point. They may be highly reliable. It may not matter much whether you, Mike, or Jason stuffs the envelopes with the surveys or launches the website with the survey monkey. But do people's answers to survey questions actually reflect the reality of their lives and views? This is the issue of the validity of a method. Maybe the question was poorly worded and lots of people didn't understand it. Maybe it was well worded, but only for people from particular social backgrounds and contexts. (Think here of the criticisms of cultural bias in the standardized tests for college admission, such as the ACT and SAT tests.) Maybe the question wasn't culturally biased but implied a certain appropriate answer. Maybe the very order of the questions implied a certain appropriate response, leading people along, perhaps to the answers the researchers were hoping to get to support a certain academic point of view. Or maybe a person's real views were way too complex to fit into the options and scales of the survey. Maybe the person had poor reading skills. Maybe their native language is different from the one the survey uses. Maybe the person responded more with an eye to making themselves or their social relations look good, rather than with what they actually think. And on and on and on.

Fieldwork, on the other hand, tends to be much higher in validity. You can tailor the wording of questions to the person and clear up any confusions they might express. (Don't we always take our knowledge of the other person into account when we frame any question we might ask of them?) You can observe them expressing the views they have without asking any questions at all. (Here is the great power of participant observation: You can watch and listen as people interact with others in a social context, with little or no prompting from you.) You can hear back from people in your fieldwork situation about what are the best questions to ask, what are the best ways to frame them, and what people's responses actually mean. (Participatory research to the rescue!)

So a standard maxim in methodology is that quantitative survey research is high in reliability and low in validity, while qualitative fieldwork is low in reliability and high in validity. By and large we agree with this maxim. So too do the large number of scholars who are increasingly trying ***mixed methods*** that combine quantitative and qualitative measures, hoping to build on the strengths of both to overcome each of their weaknesses. We very much applaud this trend.[1]

But we also want to make a few clarifications that come from appreciating the contextuality and interactivity of fieldwork methods. In a sense, fieldwork methods are actually highly reliable—once you take into account the full contexuality (and intercontexuality) of the research encounter. Jason changes a bit day by day, like all of us, and so too do the settings in Boystown that he observed in his fieldwork. But not all that much. Each day's fieldwork generally shows much the same results. We just have to consider that Jason, a gay man, will likely have different interactions and insights into those settings to Mike, a heterosexual man, in those same settings.

And the validity of fieldwork is not as easily attained as the standard maxim seems to imply. Although Jason and Mike probably come back from each new day's fieldwork with results that are similar to those of the previous day, their differences in likely findings suggest that they would in part be measuring themselves, not only the fieldwork's settings. In order to make the results valid in the sense of being sure they reflect the realities of the lives of the They, the We has to take the You into account.

So the differences we are hypothesizing between Mike and Jason doing the same work in the same research settings suggest that, in fieldwork, we do not get literal truth from our results. It matters who is doing the fieldwork. And that's not necessarily a bad thing. It means that a researcher's perspective and how others interact with him or her enable us to look at different sides of the same social situation: the "jewel" metaphor of truth that we've spoken about in earlier chapters. This potential for achieving "positive bias" (another term from earlier in the book) depends in part on valuing our differences—both differences between researchers and those between researchers and participants. Even Jason as a gay man studying other gay men had many, many points of difference and purpose from the gay men in the social settings he studied in Boystown. He was still a "stranger" to them—just a different kind of stranger to the stranger Mike would be. The epistemological power of qualitative fieldwork comes from appreciating the value (and thus the values) of our varying marginal positions to the situations we study.

Ecologists sometimes talk about the edge of a lake as its "littoral" zone. If we can be excused the pun, qualitative fieldwork does not give us literal truth; it gives us ***littoral truth***—truth from the margins, near but not too near, far but not too far.[2] Which is a very, very valuable truth to attain. We just have to be sure we understand what and where that margin is, so we can appreciate the perspective it gives us on the center of the fieldwork "lake."

One of the best features of littoral truth is its capacity for surprise. Survey methods do not generally yield littoral truths unless the survey is generated, conducted, and analyzed through participatory methods that bring the near and the far together. Survey methods generally take place from far away, which makes the features of social life more easily objectified and stereotyped. We think we know, and we tend to use broad categories that stabilize variation by allocating everything into a few large boxes. But when the You is closer in, it is hard not to be impressed with how little we know. Yes, one day's fieldwork is likely much like the previous—but not always! Sometimes you come back zinging with "Wow!" and "I had no idea." Take this as a truism of fieldwork: People are complex. And they are creative, constantly juggling the demands and opportunities they face, searching for new solutions. Sometimes they find them, and the social theory that made sense in a previous decade no longer seems so apt. The field researcher is close enough to the spark and tinder of real social life that very often she or he can see the change underway, or at least its first small flames.

Which puts another spin on the lower reliability often attributed to fieldwork methods and why we are a bit cautious of accepting that characterization. We often hear that the goal of science is predictability. Indeed, there is much value is having a good sense of the regularities of life, to better navigate successfully through them. But much of what any of us are doing in that navigation is looking for the different tacks through the storms than others have taken, as our own social position is never exactly the same as another's. So we seek an understanding of sameness in order to do something different. With fieldwork, you get a chance to ride on another's ship for a moment, watching their technique at the wheelhouse, being given a chance to see the maps they use, and talking to them, amid the howling of the wind, about how they gained those techniques and gathered those maps. In short, you never know for sure what you will learn and what your work will contribute to the questions that the We have about social life and where it is going. The lower reliability attributed to fieldwork is thus one of its greatest strengths.

The Promise for the You

And one of its greatest pleasures for You, the researcher. The creativity you encounter in your fieldwork lends creativity to your research too. As Mike likes to say, if you have all the answers, you don't have all the questions.[3] The interactivity of fieldwork constantly presents you with new questions—if you are open to hearing them. Consequently, most researchers find that their project changes considerably during the course of fieldwork. The methods change, even the topic changes.

For example, when Mike began the work that later became *Childerley*, his plan was to do a comparative study of how people in England and New England valued landscape, looking at an exurban village in each region. But, yow! They sure had plenty to say in the village in England. Mike had more than enough to write about just on "Childerley" (the village's pseudonym). Plus, the more Mike listened to what people had to say there, the more he felt that national differences were much less interesting than the differences across social class he kept encountering in this English fieldwork. Mike hadn't gone into the project thinking much about class (which he finds naïve in retrospect). But it hit him over the head time and again right in the first weeks of his research. So he changed his method and dropped the international comparison.

Mike also changed his topic. He came to realize that the question he began with—values for landscape—had a built-in class bias. Middle-class and wealthy villagers in Childerley loved to talk about landscape and could go on about it at considerable length. Working-class villagers were certainly familiar with the word and the idea but showed little interest in it and had a limited cultural vocabulary for describing the visual appeal of landscape. They had lots to say about nature, though, such as where in the local area they had had interesting encounters and interactions with what they considered nature. They also had lots to say about their family history in the village and their family traditions of being "country people" who live close to nature—farming, gardening, and hunting, and cooking and eating foods got from these activities. After getting to know these villagers—including making lifelong friends of Kath and Doug—Mike concluded that he had framed his research question from his own class perspective. So instead of an international comparison of the value of landscape, he switched his focus to looking at the relationship between ideas of nature and social class in England.

Mike's doctoral committee was a bit baffled by the change at first, and we strongly encourage faculties to lighten up a bit in their guidance of students. Expect the unexpected. Proposal defenses are all too often taken as a kind of contract, and student researchers in particular, given their lower position in the academic hierarchy, often feel a sense of alarm when it becomes plain that things are not turning out as they were described in the proposal. The same problem can beset the more senior researcher too, trying to fulfill what he or she proposed in a grant. Use your social skills to ease through these restrictions. You'll almost certainly be finding your way to better science.

Here's another little maxim: If your research questions and methods remain exactly the same at the end of your fieldwork, you didn't need to do the research to begin with. You already knew the answer. Which means not only that you didn't make much of a contribution to science but also that you denied yourself the incredible opportunity for personal growth that fieldwork can provide.

Some of that opportunity for growth comes from making great friends, as Mike did with Kath and Doug. OK, you may still make good friends in the field even if your ideas don't change much during the work. But generally the best friendships come through mutual learning in our encounters. Open yourself up more to what participants tell you and you'll build closer ties as you deepen your understanding.

Older guides to methods often cautioned about making friends with your participants, though. Many a field researcher has been admonished about the danger of "going native" and losing the social distance that traditional norms of objectivity encourage. Who criticizes their own friends and kin, after all? But think about it for half a second. Does one really never criticize one's friends and kin? If you care about them, you certainly do criticize them, as well as being critical of the situations that cause their troubles. Yes, of course, we are often highly critical of those we don't like or don't know very well. But these negative social relations of critique seem to hold equal, if not greater, potential for distorting our impressions of the world and warping the data we gather both in fieldwork research and in the fieldwork of daily life.

The problem is not whether to make friends with your research participants. The problem is whether you are able to maintain a critical eye about their doings and situations. Keeping one foot on the margins and maintaining the stranger's littoral truth, even as you extend out into the lake, should help you hold onto that critical position while making friends in the field. It can be a balancing act and you may wish you had longer legs! Sometimes you may stumble one way or the other. But those moments of stumble often lead to good friendships and good insights, both.

It's all part of the adventure of fieldwork. Since we ordinarily don't find exactly what we expect, we grow with each strange encounter and result. Fieldwork can be confusing and frustrating, as we said at the beginning of the chapter. It can be lonely and personally challenging. But it is seldom dull.[4] And that, more than any other reason, may be why so many scholars now embrace fieldwork despite its difficulties and the clearer path to results and publications that quantitative methods generally provide.

The Promise for the They

Moreover, with fieldwork methods, there is a high chance of actually making a real contribution to real lives. Maybe not a huge contribution, but surely a more direct and intimate one than with a survey or a model based on government census data. On the one hand, the researcher gets directly involved in people's lives and concerns, especially when the work has a participatory dimension to it. Those great friendships are very often as meaningful for participants as they are for researchers. And you wind up helping out in small ways with people's daily lives, sometimes leading to big changes for them. For example, Hakim Hasan, the outdoor book vendor who became one of Mitch Duneier's key participants in *Sidewalk* and who Duneier went on to teach a course with at the University of California-Santa Barbara, isn't selling books on the street anymore. At the time of writing, Hasan is director of the Metropolitan Institute at the Metropolitan College of New York—a change in his life that directly resulted from his engagement with Duneier.

On the other hand, there can be important indirect benefits for participants. Fieldwork tends to be problem-focused, again especially when it has a participatory dimension. Duneier's *Sidewalk* undercut the scientific credibility of the "broken windows" theory of crime and the "stop-and-frisk" policing that Mayors Giuliani and Bloomberg instituted based on it. Duneier was not alone. Many other studies undercut it too and activists against racial profiling have worked hard to end the practice. They now seem to be getting somewhere. The new mayor of New York, Bill de Blasio, has pledged to reform "stop-and-frisk." Social science, working together with activists, made a real difference in real lives.

Plus fieldwork is generally far more accessible for a broader We—a We that also includes the They of participants in the audience. Mike still treasures the words of a farmer who said of Mike's *Farming for Us All*: "[It]changed my life. I'm a completely different farmer now." Mike's book also contained some arguments about social theory that Mike still likes very much. That's not what the farmer was talking about. He was talking about the book's accounts of farmers facing the struggles of reaching for sustainability in an economy that seldom seems to reward it. Yes, the book had little nuggets of abstraction of the sort that specialists enjoy. But for those for whom those nuggets were more like bits of grit, there was plenty else in the book to appreciate. As we discussed in the previous chapter, the vividness of fieldwork lends itself to this more open conception of science's role and science's audience.

That openness to including the They in the We promotes the multilogical strength of fieldwork methods. Fulfilling these promises for the They also fulfills them for You as well. It makes it more likely that your work will have the relevance you want it to have, bringing the logics of science together with the logics of practice. It makes it more likely that your multilogical conversations with participants will give you confidence that your work is accurate and original, informed as it is by their local knowledge and creative responses to their context. And, as we've said, a multilogical approach makes it more likely you will develop meaningful and lasting ties with your participants. Work that is relevant, accurate, original, and meaningful is what the We wants too.

In short, when we fulfill the promise for the They, we fulfill it for You and for We as well. That triple consciousness: All these voices are all our voices.

* * *

We hope that you come away from this book feeling invited not just to give fieldwork a try but also to appreciate what the philosopher Mikhail Bakhtin liked to call "unfinalizability." We've come now to the end of this book, its very final paragraph. But although books have endings, the multilogical character of fieldwork teaches us that there are no last words. To accept triple consciousness is also to accept that there are no final truths—except, perhaps, the final truth that there aren't any final truths, at least when we approach our work with an openness to the wonder of the unknown. Which, after all, is the only reason to do research.

NOTES

Chapter 1 The Multilogical Approach

1. Bell 1993.
2. We know of at least two other strikingly similar stories from job talks gone bad.
3. Bland & Bell 2007 and Bell et al. 2011.
4. For a longer discussion of the multilogical character of social life—a discussion which is itself multiple in that it comes out of a debate among 10 scholars—see Bell et al. (2011).
5. Weber 1978 [1922: 4].
6. Weber 1978 [1922: 8].
7. Weber 2001 [1919: 7].
8. Weber (1978) [1922: 9].
9. His biographers, at least, largely agree.
10. Weber 1978 [1922: 9–10].
11. A popular example of this broader, almost encyclopedic approach is Berg's *Qualitative Research Methods for the Social Sciences*, now in its 8th edition.
12. Examples include the *Sage Handbook of Interview Research, Digital Qualitative Research Methods, Using Narrative in Research, Handbook of Feminist Research, Critical Ethnography*, and *All You Need to Know About Action Research*, to cite some recent titles or new editions.
13. A classic example of this approach is Becker's *Tricks of the Trade: How to Think About Your Research While You're Doing It*, published by Chicago in 1998 but still popular and widely recommended. "Why to" books generally speak with a punchy and personal style that engage the reader in a conversation, thus inviting the reader's own creative capacities. They are also typically short. But some "why to" books take a more encyclopedic approach, often with a duller and more professionally-oriented style, such as Denzin and Lincoln's *Landscape of Qualitative Research* and their *Strategies of Qualitative Inquiry*, both of which were released in their third editions by Sage in 2007, and both of which are quite long (632 and 440 pages, respectively).
14. This book does not cover, for example, historical methods and methods of material interpretation such as an archeologist routinely must do, among other important qualitative methods.

Chapter 2 The *They* Voice: Participants and Communities

1. Bland & Bell 2007.
2. Tavory & Timmermans 2009.

3. This term was first suggested by Gayatri Chakravorty Spivak, who later retracted her commitment to the phrase. But it has since become commonplace.
4. McCall 2005.
5. Brubaker 2004.
6. Moore 2011.
7. Orne 2011, 2013.

Chapter 3 The *You* Voice: Researchers

1. Devault 1990.
2. Simmel 1908.
3. Simmel 1908.
4. Agar 1996.
5. Since his first name appeared on the list of pseudonyms he was drawing from, he likes to joke that he was actually the 14th participant in the study.
6. Devault 1990.

Chapter 4 The *We* Voice: The Audience

1. Bakhtin 1984.
2. Here we build out from—in the spirit, we believe, of "extending"—Michael Burawoy's 1998 notion of "extended" in his account of the "extended case method."
3. For more on "strange explanation," see Bell et al. (2011).

Chapter 5 Listening: Interview Methods

1. Mike later re-interviewed Sir Maynard, however.
2. For more on truth as a multifaceted and ever-changing jewel, see Bell (forthcoming, 2016).
3. Guest, Bunce, & Johnson 2006.
4. Johnson et al. 2010.
5. Bell 1994.
6. Duneier 1999.
7. Brown-Saracino 2010.
8. Simmel 1908.
9. González-López 2005.
10. We prefer the phrase "co-constructed" to "semi-structured" to emphasize the collaborative spirit of this form of interviewing.
11. From Sharp 2008.
12. MacLean et al. 2004.

Chapter 6 Looking: Ethnographic Observation

1. For another example of the difficulties of drink in gaining ethnographic acceptance, see Mike's experiences of trying to keep up with British farm workers doing "rounds" drinking, as reported in Bell (1994: 61–62).
2. Goffman 1959.
3. Fine 2008.
4. Flyvbjerg 2006.
5. Charmaz 2006.

6. Orne (forthcoming, 2015).
7. Collins 2009.
8. Drake & Cayton 1970 [1945].
9. This term was introduced by Duneier (1999), based on his reading of the work of the sociological polymath, Howard Becker.
10. For details, see Bell (2004: 132–139).
11. Maynard 2003.
12. "Key informants" is the standard term, but is based on a positivistic metaphor of spying that we regard as inappropriate for what really goes on in fieldwork.
13. Personal communication. See Western (1992 and 2012).
14. Geertz 1973.
15. Emerson, Fretz, & Shaw 2010.

Chapter 7 Participating: Research as Practice

1. This scene is drawn from the research reported in Lyon et al. (2010), but also includes some evidence not reported there.
2. We conducted this search of *Sociological Abstracts* on May 20, 2014, entering "participatory research" in quotes to ensure it was treated as a single phrase, and searching with "anywhere" selected.
3. We did this search the same day as the above. The total number of hits for all years was 2937.
4. Bentley & Werner 1991, Bentley et al. 1994, and Bentley 2006.
5. Stoecker 2005: 6.
6. Ashwood et al. 2014.
7. Mills 1959.
8. See Bell (2004, 2012, and forthcoming). These issues are widely recognized in the scholarly literature, although this language is not commonly used. Selection is basically a restating of what is sometimes called the "weak critique" in the sociology of science and reflection is basically a restating of the "strong critique." To put it another way, selection is Kuhn and Merton and reflection is Durkheim and Foucault.
9. Arnstein 1969.
10. Cooke & Kothari 2001: 14 and Hayward, Simpson, & Wood 2004: 95.
11. Lee 2007.
12. Lyon et al. 2010: 555.
13. Lyon et al. 2010: 553.
14. Lyon et al. 2010: 553.
15. Parker 2011.
16. Barringer 2008.
17. Steiner et al. 2008: 86.
18. Botkin 2001: 68.
19. Wacquant 2004.
20. Scheper-Hughes 1992.
21. Myerhoff 1978.
22. These opportunities led Hasan to give up street vending. As of May, 2014, he is Director of the Metropolitan Institute at Metropolitan College of New York.
23. This was in 2000 at Iowa State University.
24. On the Practical Farmers of Iowa, see Bell (2004).
25. Skloot 2010: 1–2.
26. Ellis 1995 and 2004.
27. Myerhoff 1978: 228.

28. Du Bois 1903: 11.
29. Spitz et al. (unpublished manuscript).
30. Ellis 1999.

Chapter 8 The Multilogics of Writing

1. Belcher 2009.
2. Hagger-Johnson et al. 2013.
3. Somerville 2013.
4. Harper 2005: 38.
5. Bell 2011.
6. Stassart et al. 2011.
7. The actual quote from Mussorgsky, which is widely available on the web, is: "Art is not an end in itself, but a means of addressing humanity." We have not been able to track down the original source, however.
8. Geertz 1973.
9. Bell 1994: 3.
10. Rowling 1999: 1.
11. Phelan, Link, & Feldman 2013: 167.

Chapter 9 The Promise of Fieldwork

1. For an introduction to the great potential of mixed methods, see Johnson and Onwuegbuzie (2004) and Johnson et al. (2007), as well as the *Journal of Mixed Methods Research*.
2. See Bell (2004) for the original coining of this pun, derived from his reading of Simmel (1908).
3. Bell 2011.
4. And if it is, or has become so, it's time to switch topics or come on home and start writing.

REFERENCES

Agar, Michael H. (1996). *The Professional Stranger: An Informal Introduction to Ethnography*. San Diego, CA: Academic Press.

Arnstein, Sherrie R. (1969). "A Ladder of Citizen Participation." *American Institute of Planners Journal* 35(4), 216–224.

Ashwood, Loka, Noelle Harden, Michael M. Bell, & William Bland (2014). "Linked and Situated: Grounded Knowledge." *Rural Sociology*. Early View publication online, March 14, 2014.

Bakhtin, Mikhail (1984) [1965]. *Rabelais and His World*. Bloomington, IN: Indiana University Press.

Barringer, Felicity (2008). "Calvin L. Beale, Demographer With a Feel for Rural America, Dies at 85." *New York Times*, September 2. Retrieved May 25, 2014 from www.nytimes.com.

Becker, Howard S. (1998). *Tricks of the Trade: How to Think about Your Research While You're Doing It*. Chicago, IL: University of Chicago Press.

Becker, H. S. (2008). *Writing for social scientists: How to start and finish your thesis, book, or article*. Chicago, IL: University of Chicago Press.

Belcher, Wendy L. (2009). *Writing Your Journal Article in 12 Weeks: A Guide to Academic Publishing Success*. Thousand Oaks, CA: Sage Publications.

Bell, Michael M. (1994). *Childerley: Nature and Morality in a Country Village*. Chicago, IL: University of Chicago Press.

Bell, Michael M. 2011. "If You Have All the Answers, You Don't Have All the Questions," in Michael M. Bell et al., *The Strange Music of Social Life: A Dialogue on Dialogic Sociology*. Ann Goetting, ed. Philadelphia, PA: Temple University Press.

Bell, Michael M. (2012). *An Invitation to Environmental Sociology*. 4th edition. Thousand Oaks, CA: Pine Forge Press (Sage).

Bell, Michael M. (forthcoming 2016.) *An Ancient Triangle: Nature, Faith, and Community*. Princeton, NJ: Princeton University Press.

Bell, Michael M., with Donna Bauer, Sue Jarnagin, & Greg Peter (2004). *Farming for Us All: Practical Agriculture and the Cultivation of Sustainability*. Rural Studies Series of the Rural Sociological Society. College Station, PA: Penn State University Press.

Bell, Michael M., with Andrew Abbott, Judith Blau, Diana Crane, Stacy Holman Jones, Shamus Kahn, Vanina Leschziner, John Levi Martin, Christopher McRae, Marc Steinberg, & John Chappell Stowe (2011). *The Strange Music of Social Life: A Dialogue on Dialogic Sociology*. Ann Goetting, ed. Philadelphia, PA: Temple University Press.

Bentley, Jeffery W. (2006). "Folk Experiments." *Agriculture and Human Values* 23(4): 451–461.

Bentley, Jeffery W. & Werner Melara (1991). "Experimenting with Honduran Farmer-Experimenters." *Overseas Development Institute Newsletter* 24(June): 31–48.

Bentley, Jeffery W., G. Rodriguez, & A. Gonzalez (1994). "Science and People: Honduran Compesinos and Natural Pest Control Inventions." *Agriculture and Human Values* 11(2/3): 178–182.

Berg, Bruce L. (2011) *Qualitative Research Methods for the Social Sciences*. 8th edition. Harlow, UK: Pearson Education.

Bland, William L. & Michael M. Bell (2007). "A Holon Approach to Agroecology." *International Journal of Agricultural Sustainability* 5(4): 280–294.

Botkin, Daniel B (2001). *No Man's Garden: Thoreau And A New Vision For Civilization And Nature*. Washington, DC: Island Press.

Brown-Saracino, J. (2010). *A Neighborhood That Never Changes*. Chicago, IL: University of Chicago Press.

Brubaker, Rogers (2004). *Ethnicity Without Groups*. Cambridge, MA: Harvard University Press.

Burawoy, Michael (1998). "The Extended Case Method." *Sociological Theory* 16(1): 4–33.

Charmaz, K. (2006). *Constructing Grounded Theory*. SAGE: Thousand Oaks.

Collins, Jane L. 2009. *Threads*. Chicago, IL: University of Chicago Press.

Cooke, Bill & Uma Kothari, eds. (2001). *Participation: The New Tyranny?* London: Zed Books.

Devault, Marjorie L. (1990). "Talking and Listening from Women's Standpoint: Feminist Strategies for Interviewing and Analysis." *Social Problems* 37(1): 96–116.

Drake, Saint Clair, and Horace Cayton (1970) [1945]. *Black Metropolis*. Chicago, IL: University of Chicago Press.

Du Bois, W. E. B. (1999) [1903]. *The Souls of Black Folk*. New York: Norton.

Duneier, Mitchell (1999). *Sidewalk*. New York: Farrar, Straus, and Giroux.

Ellis, Carolyn (1995). *Final Negotiations: A Story of Love, Loss, and Chronic Illness*. Philadelphia, PA: Temple University Press.

Ellis, Carolyn (1999). "Heartful Autoethnography." *Qualitative Health Research* 9(5): 669–683.

Ellis, Carolyn (2004). *The Ethnographic I: A Methodological Novel about Autoethnography*. Walnut Creek, CA: AltaMira Press.

Ellis, C. (2009). "Autoethnography as Method (review)". *Biography* 32(2).

Emerson, R. M., R. I. Fretz, & L. L. Shaw (2010). *Writing Ethnographic Fieldnotes*. Chicago, IL: University of Chicago Press.

Fine, Gary Allen (2008). *Kitchens*. Berkeley, CA: University of California Press.

Flyvbjerg, B. (2006). "Five misunderstandings about case-study research." *Qualitative Inquiry* 12(2).

Geertz, C. (1973). "Deep Play: Notes on the Balinese Cockfight" in *The Interpretation of Cultures*. New York: Basic Books.

Geertz, Clifford (1973). "Thick Description: Toward an Interpretive Theory of Culture," in *The Interpretation of Cultures*. New York: Basic Books.

Glaser, Barney & Anselm Strauss (1967). *The Discovery of Grounded Theory*. Chicago: Aldine.

Goffman, Erving (1959). *The Presentation of Self in Everyday Life*. Garden City, NY: Doubleday.

González-López, Gloria (2005). *Erotic Journeys*. Berkeley, CA: University of California Press.

Guest, G., A. Bunce, & L. Johnson (2006). "How Many Interviews Are Enough?: An Experiment with Data Saturation and Variability," *Field Methods* 18(1): 59–82.

Hagger-Johnson, G., P. Hegarty, & M. Barker (2013). "Public Engagement, Knowledge Transfer, and Impact Validity." *Journal of Social Issues* 69(4): 664–683.

Harper, Douglas (2005). "An Argument for Visual Sociology," in Jon Prosser, ed., *Image-Based Research: A Sourcebook for Qualitative Researchers*, London and Philadelphia: Routledge,.

Hayward, C., L. Simpson, & L. Wood (2004). "Still Left Out in the Cold: Problematising Participatory Research and Development." *Sociologia Ruralis* 44(1): 95–108.

Johnson, C. V., M. J. Mimiaga, S. L. Reisner, A. M. Tetu, & K. H. Mayer (2010). "The Use of Respondent-driven Sampling to Recruit At-risk Minority Men Who Have Sex with Men in Massachusetts." *Journal of Gay & Lesbian Social Services* 22(4): 476–494.

Johnson, R. Burke and Anthony J. Onwuegbuzie (2004). "Mixed Methods Research: A Research Paradigm Whose Time Has Come." *Educational Researcher* 33(7): 14–26.

Johnson, R. Burke, Anthony J. Onwuegbuzie and Lisa A. Turner (2007). "Toward a Definition of Mixed Methods Research." *Journal of Mixed Methods Research* 1(2): 112–133.

Lee, Carolyn (2007). "Is There a Place for Private Conversation in Public Dialogue? Comparing Stakeholder Assessments of Informal Communication in Collaborative Regional Planning." *American Journal of Sociology* 113(1): 41–96.

Lyon, Alexandra, Michael M. Bell, Nora Swan Croll, Randall Jackson, & Claudio Gratton (2010). "Maculate Conceptions: Power, Process, and Creativity in Participatory Research." *Rural Sociology* 75(4): 538–559.

McCall, Leslie. (2005). "The Complexity of Intersectionality." *Signs: Journal of Women in Culture and Society* 30(3), 1771–1800.

MacLean, L., M. Meyer, & A. Estable (2004). "Improving Accuracy of Transcripts in Qualitative Research." *Qualitative Health Research* 14(1): 113–123.

Maynard, Doug W. (2003). *Bad News, Good News: Conversational Order in Everyday Talk and Clinical Settings*. Chicago, IL: University of Chicago Press.

Mills, C. Wright (1959). *The Sociological Imagination*. New York: Grove.

Moore, Mignon (2011). *Invisible Families*. Berkeley, CA: University of California Press.

Myerhoff, Barbara (1978). *Number Our Days*. New York: Simon and Schuster.

Nordqvist, P. (2012). "'I Don't Want Us to Stand Out More than We Already Do': Complexities and Negotiations in Lesbian Couples' Accounts of Becoming a Family through Donor Conception." *Sexualities* 15(5/6): 644–661.

Orne, Jason (2011). "You Will Always Have to 'Out' Yourself: Reconsidering Coming Out Through Strategic Outness." *Sexualities* 14(6): 681–703.

Orne, Jason (2013). "Queers in the Line of Fire: Goffman's Stigma Revisited." *The Sociological Quarterly* 54(2): 229–253.

Orne, Jason (forthcoming, 2015). *Boystown*. Chicago, IL: University of Chicago Press.

Parker, Timothy (2011). "More than 50 Years of Service." *USDA Blog*. Retrieved May 25, 2014 from http://blogs.usda.gov.

Phelan, Jo C., Bruce G. Link, & Naumi M. Feldman (2013). "The Genomic Revolution and Beliefs about Essential Racial Differences: A Backdoor to Eugenics?" *American Sociological Review* 78(2): 167–191.

Rowling, J. K. (1999). *Harry Potter and the Sorcerer's Stone*. New York: Scholastic.

Scheper-Hughes, Nancy (1992). *Death without Weeping: The Violence of Everyday Life in Brazil*. Berkeley, CA: University of California Press.

Sharp, Shane (2008). "A Short Course on Interviewing." Unpublished manuscript.

Simmel, Georg (1971 [1908]. "The Stranger," in Donald N. Levine, ed., *On Individuality and Social Forms: Selected Writings*. Chicago, IL: University of Chicago Press.

Skloot, Rebecca (2010). *The Immortal Life of Henrietta Lacks*. New York: Random House.

Somerville, M. (2013). *Water in a Dry Land*. London: Routledge.

Spitz, Gina, Jason Orne, & Michael M. Bell. "Goffman and a Deck of Cards: The Trick of Power." Unpublished manuscript.

Stassart, Pierre Marie, Valerie Mathieu, & Francois Melard (2011). "Reflexive Audiovisual Methodology: The Emergence of 'Minority Practices' Among Pluriactive Stock Farmers." *Journal of Rural Studies* 27(4): 403–413.

Steiner, Daniel, Heinz J. Zumbühl, & Andreas Bauder (2008). "Two Alpine Glaciers over the Past Two Centuries: A Scientific View Based on Pictorial Sources," in Orlove, B., Wiegandt, E., & B. H Luckman, eds., *Darkening Peaks: Glacier Retreat, Science, and Society*. Berkeley, Los Angeles, and London: University of California Press.

Stoecker, Randy (2005). *Research Methods for Community Change: A Project-Based Approach*. Thousand Oaks, CA: Sage Publications.

Tavory, Iddo & S. Timmermans (2009). "Two Cases of Ethnography: Grounded Theory and the Extended Case Method." *Ethnography* 10(3): 243–263.

Wacquant, Loïc (2004). *Body and Soul: Notebooks of an Apprentice Boxer*. New York: Oxford University Press.

Weber, Max (1978) [1922]. *Economy and Society: An Outline of Interpretive Sociology*. Berkeley, CA: University of California Press.

Weber, Max (2001) [1919]. *From Max Weber: Essays in Sociology*. H. H. Gerth & C. Wright Mills, eds. Oxford, UK: Routledge.

Western, John (1992). *A Passage to England: Barbadian Londoners Speak of Home*. Minneapolis, MN: University of Minnesota Press.

Western, John (2012). *Cosmopolitan Europe: A Strasbourg Self-Portrait*. Burlington, VT: Ashgate.

Glossary Index

C

D

M

N

O